I Can Do It!
I Can Do It!

I Can Do It! I Can Do It!

135 Successful
Independent Learning Activities

By LaBritta Gilbert
Photographs by Russell Gilbert

Gryphon House Inc.
Mt. Rainier, Maryland

© 1984 by LaBritta Gilbert

ISBN 0-87659-107-1

Published by Gryphon House, Inc.,
3706 Otis Street,
Mt. Rainier, Maryland 20712

Design: Cynthia Fowler

Typesetting: Lithocomp

Photographs on pages 17, 18, 19, 21, 22, 27, 28, 30, 31, 32, 34, 35,
36, 38, 39 and 40 were taken by Robert Palmer of Photographics,
Houston, Texas.

To Russell and Michael

Prologue

LEARNING:

may be untidy
is fragile
defines us
is often unorthodox
(irreverent, too)
may be inconvenient
is not sitting still
is not being quiet
is letting something inside out
wonders
makes mistakes
makes sense
makes no sense

waits on self-esteem: I learn only as much as I think I deserve to know.

It also:
may arrive unannounced
won't be put off
is play
is work
is frustration
is necessary
feels right
hurts sometimes
changes us
can be diverted but not denied
is a skeptic
needs space
needs time
asks forbearance
can't be taught
can't be caught
knows
guesses
guesses wrong
(and knows it's all right)
has many disguises
believes
never stops.

The Bear's Story

The small boy's name is not important to the story. But he had a toy Koala whose name was poetry. It was Fred Paul Bear, Whose Nickname is Pierre. The boy gave the name matter-of-factly whenever he was asked, and people nodded knowingly. And all was well. Then the two of them took a trip with relatives and something significant happened. Fred Paul Bear, Whose Nickname is Pierre's name was changed. The boy was changed, too, but I'm not sure just how. Maybe he stopped believing in poetry—I don't know. It happened in a restaurant when they were having lunch with their family. A waitress asked the bear's name and laughed loudly when the boy said, "Fred Paul Bear, Whose Nickname is Pierre." Well, a silence fell on that table, and as the party was leaving the restaurant, the boy solemnly announced the bear's new name: Fluffy. Nobody laughed.

Foreword to Teachers

Do you ever feel like the reluctant star of your own show, while a still voice somewhere inside insists that learning should be in the hands of the learners? If you do, your classroom may be a candidate for a transformation via individualization, the way mine was. I loved school, but I seemed to be the only one in the class who felt that way! My students didn't actually dislike school; there was just a certain blandness to our days. Besides, I was uncomfortable with the way they always seemed to look to me to perform. And those were my good days; on bad days too much sitting and following directions prompted outright mutiny. What has gone wrong when intense student involvement just doesn't happen the way our instructors promised, anyway? Very likely the students are not participating fully enough in their own education. This situation can be reversed, as I learned, by relinquishing center stage to them.

A chance observation of an individualized preschool program in action turned my teaching career completely around. I was so excited by what I'd seen that I couldn't wait to try it with my own class. The change was nothing short of miraculous. I was never again the same teacher, and later I directed my own individualized school. It was a living kaleidoscope. Here was a clear example of less being more. Less teacher involvement equaled more student involvement.

You see, once activated, this principle is beautifully self-perpetuating: a child's driving force is to find out all there is to know about everything. Capitalize on that and you unleash learning potential that is boundless! Set it in motion by making it possible for children to answer many of their own questions. Individualized activities are one way to do this. They are avenues to information about a wide variety of things, and children can draw conclusions by using their own senses, especially the sense of touch. Everything is grist for the mill: everyday activities, mundane to adults who have performed them countless times, are soul-satisfying experiences to children performing them for the first time. Every type of material, every object and substance which might serve to broaden experience suddenly seems full of promise: is this a new or rarely-experienced feel? sound? manipulative challenge? Is it a material never seen before, or never seen at close range and for as long as one likes? Is it a fascinating gadget usually used by fathers and mothers?

Sometimes you can almost read the thoughts of a child absorbed with an exercise: "So that's how that's done!" "So that's how that works!" Some of my favorite exercises are those which demystify scientific principles for children by introducing them to objects and substances found in their own homes, but which are unfamiliar to them. Nothing is sacred to dedicated "individualists"; if it works, we want them to see how! We become obsessed with letting them in on every little secret in the universe. Our credo becomes *let them use their hands*. Our business becomes contriving ways to make it happen.

It seems to me that the undisputed masters of individualized learning techniques are teachers of the Montessori method of education. I learned the fundamentals of individualization and how to implement it in my own classroom by attending several excellent Montessori-sponsored workshops. During one on teacher-made materials, I made enough exercises to introduce individualization to my class. However, they were not adequate in number either to fill my newly-constructed shelves or to satisfy my new expectations, and though commercial materials were available, they were financially out of reach.

Pondering this, I remembered some "individualized activities" from the past which I had created on-the-spot, in non-teaching situations, and long before I had heard the term. The first of these had been born of the desperation of the moment: how to entertain a friend's three-year-old without any toys at hand. (This was before my own children were born.) A quick search through my apartment kitchen had yielded pots, pans, and measuring utensils. A bag of dried split peas completed the activity, and to my surprise and relief it occupied my little charge for the better part of an afternoon. When I later had toddlers of my own, "measuring peas" was a staple play activity for them. On one occasion, some broken sets of colorful buttons, bought in a frantic moment from a bargain bin in a fabric store, kept both children occupied while I completed my purchases. The buttons were such a favorite that I later kept them and a muffin tin in the car and they fascinated anew each time I brought them out, and kept the peace during many traffic jams. In those days a kitchen baster in the bathtub seemed to make perfect sense, and one rainy day the wonder of a saltine cracker expanding in water provided me with a few moments of much-needed still and quiet.

I thought perhaps I could now draw on these past experiences to help equip my classroom. Why wouldn't they be just as useful now as they had been then? Weren't they true individualized activities? I decided they were. Now with the principle of individualization firmly fixed in my mind, ideas began to jump out at me from everywhere; exercises seemed to invent themselves. Some suggested themselves as adaptations of teaching materials which we all have long considered teaching standbys. I simply dressed them differently—by using unfamiliar materials in familiar ways, or old materials in new ways, I hoped to get children to take a closer look, and it seemed to work.

If individualized learning is new to you, let me assure you it is as old as learning itself. It is as ancient as a cave child examining an unusual rock, and as contemporary as today's children touching everything within reach at the supermarket.

An individualized exercise consists of three-dimensional objects to be manipulated by the user. Each exercise has a single function. An exercise to introduce magnetic attraction, for example, would consist of a magnet and various objects to test for magnetic attraction. Through using the actual objects, students experience firsthand what a magnet will and won't do. (And will it behave the same way tomorrow?) These activities are used for as long as desired, and repeated as often as desired, by individual students. What other kind of lesson on magnetism could possibly rival holding a magnet in one's own hands and experiencing its mysterious forces? This is individualized learning—experimentation and exploration at an unhurried pace. In our rush toward ever more sophisticated teaching devices, we often forget what unique learning experiences can be provided by everyday materials found in the home. Many of these exercises are so simple that construction of them consists of collecting unused items from around your own house. Everday objects, yes, but they represent opportunity for mastery of skills adults have had so long we don't remember acquiring them. This is individualized learning at its very best.

Making the switch from teacher-centered to child-centered teaching need not be traumatic for either teacher or child. If the process sounds exciting, but overwhelming, to you, have no fear! You can make the change gradually (and painlessly) if that is your wish. You can alter your present classroom arrangement as much or as little as you like. Even a few individualized learning exercises can enhance a traditional curriculum without radically upsetting its rhythm. They can be incorporated as free-time activities, or a scheduled block of time each day or certain days of the week can be devoted to individualized instruction. Many teachers welcome the change of pace such an arrangement offers. Of course, I think total commitment to individualized learning pays the greatest dividends, so I will encourage you throughout the book both to "think individualization" and to increase the number of individualized activities at your disposal. And I should warn you, it's easy to get "hooked." When you see the clamor of excitement a new exercise brings to your class, you probably won't be able to resist adding more and more of them. Rest easy—you can't have too many—in fact, the more the merrier.

Acknowledgements

Children first. I've learned all I know about learning from them. From one Sean L., aged 4, for instance, I learned something about *quantity* I never knew before: you should always cut sandwiches diagonally—that way "you get more". See what I mean? (It's important to know how things really are; it's important, too, to know how children *think* they are.) I feel indebted to all the children who have taught me and allowed me to learn with them. It's because of them this book exists.

The children who demonstrated the materials for our camera were a delight—so eager and capable. I'm deeply grateful to them, their parents and teachers. They are:

1. Students of the Oaks Academy, Houston, Texas; Headmistress Lila Macaluso, teachers Ronnie Snyder and Jan Gauvain, who worked far beyond the call of duty.

2. Students of the White Rock Montessori School, Dallas, Texas; Director Cindy Cave, who worked tirelessly for the perfection we both wanted.

3. Artists-and-models Mike, Kady, and Craig Dunlap, Chaney Pitzer, Isabel Reza, and Harold Brown, who pinch-hit for us and did so beautifully; Peggy and Nancy Dunlap, who assisted with photography.

Doreen Gerczak, Director of The Learning Experience, Spring, Texas, helped with preliminary photography which does not appear in the book but which contributed to its publication and for which I am grateful.

Sister Edna Ann Hebert, of St. Mary's Montessori School, Houston, Texas, (the most skilled "individualist" I know) deserves credit for many of the exercises, particularly in the LIFE ARTS section.

Thanks, also to: Walt Hauffe, of The Educational Showcase, Houston, Texas, for reading preliminary drafts and encouraging me to take the plunge; to Sally Pruit and Ginger Mitchell for possessing typing skills I lack and being mindreaders as well; to numerous family members and friends who followed the book's progress and were with me in spirit; and, poignantly, to those who labored long and loyally with me at A Special Place some time ago—I have not forgotten you—for it was during that venture that this one took root. We laughed a little and learned a lot, didn't we?

Special appreciation to Clayton Umbach for "walking me through" the publishing experience. He and Harold Hoffman, both of Gulf Publishing Company, Houston, Texas, and both longtime and dear friends, shared my excitement and gave me invaluable counsel.

Loving appreciation to my family for enduring. Their tolerance for my "kitchen experiments" and ever-mounting stacks of materials was remarkable. My son Russell was our photographer. His intuitive approach always fascinated me—and it always worked. My son Michael, the artist for several activities, was the one I turned to for advice of a creative nature, because I trust his judgement completely. I think my husband Wayne may have learned more about publishing than he ever cared to know. He translated much of the manuscript for submission via computer. More importantly, he always believed I could do it.

Finally, to Gryphon House, Inc., to whom rare good fortune led me: to Larry Rood, President, for his unflagging enthusiasm and commitment to excellence; to my editor Mary Rein, whose concepts meshed perfectly with mine; to others on the staff I don't know by name, but who helped make this book exceed all my expectations—thank you.

Table of Contents

Dexterity 45

Putting It All Together

Room Arrangement

Individualized activities need shelf space of their own, apart from toys and play equipment. If you need more shelves, 1'' × 12'' (25mm × 305mm) boards and concrete blocks make good ones. Paint them or leave them unfinished. They're flexible and can be freestanding (as dividers) or placed against walls. Whether you group DISCRIMINATION, DEXTERITY, ABC'S & 123'S, and AH-HA! together is a matter of choice, as they are all compatible, but CONSTRUCTION and LIFE ARTS need to be grouped separately.

Ordinarily, children are allowed to find work from among all the activities in the individualized section, but it may sometimes suit your purpose to emphasize one or more areas by specifying that choices be made from among only those. In that case, you'd need to have them grouped separately.

Activities must not be crowded on the shelves. Allow plenty of shelf space, so that there are several inches on either side of each one. Otherwise, materials become mixed and disorderly. The single most important thing you can do to ensure orderly shelves is to see that every single activity has its own container. Materials put on the shelf without containers are doomed to a short life! (See *STORAGE*)

The CONSTRUCTION area should be separated to contain its materials, which are inherently untidy, so arrange the shelf units to make it somewhat apart. This area needs at least two tables—a medium-sized one for COLLAGE and a large one for general use. The easel is here, and the shelves holding all the supplies. The CLAY container and boxes of JUNK, YARN, scrap wood and other discards are nearby. If your room has a sink, locate the CONSTRUCTION area near it if you can. If you're short of tables, mats won't work for CONSTRUCTION, but fortunately you can improvise. Buy hollow-core doors (one damaged side is okay) or 4' × 8' (1.22m × 2.44m) sheets of ¾'' (19mm) plywood and place them on concrete blocks, 12'' 305mm) square, stacked flat on each other to chair height, or, if you lack chairs, to sitting-on-the-floor height. Paint the tops or cover them with plastic, stapling it underneath, for protection. A half sheet of plywood will make a good COLLAGE table. A convenient addition in the CONSTRUCTION area is a small wall shelf at adult eye level to hold glue, paint, etc. so they can be quickly given when requested without taking an adult from the area. Or a high cupboard can hold them.

LIFE ARTS needs its own space, near the sink, too, so carve one out for it. These exercises can't be used on floor mats, either, so make tables if necessary, as described above. A place for hooks to hang clean-up supplies is needed, and a place to dry the towels. A small table that seats two is ideal for the SANDWICHES exercise (it can be used for other things as well), or two places can be set at a larger table.

Be sure tables are convenient to AH-HA! exercises; floor mats cannot be used for the ones which contain liquids.

Tools and Supplies

You already have around your house many of the necessary tools for making individualized exercises, and you can buy most of the basic materials from home centers, hardware stores or lumberyards. Some items come from an office supply, teacher's supply, fabric store or the housewares section of supermarkets. When you're shopping for small items, it's a good idea to buy a few extra for replacements which will be needed sooner or later.

Lumber will be one of four kinds: wooden dowels, 1'' × 2'' (2.5cm × 5cm) boards, 1'' × 10'' (2.5cm × 25.4cm) boards, or pegboard. Dowels are usually 36'' (91cm) long, but a longer length can be used. Buy wood in quantity; having materials on hand is half the battle of getting started, don't you agree? Look for straight boards. Any or all of the lumber can be cut where you buy it, either free or for a small charge, or if you have a saw at home, you can do the sawing yourself. The cuts are all simple and straight; most of the measurements are standardized, so while you're at it, you can cut several for use in other activities. Pegboard comes in whole 4' x 8' (122cm x 244cm), half, and quarter sheets. A quarter sheet will be large enough for the projects in this book. Notice, however, that pegboard comes in two thicknesses: 1/8'' (3mm) and 1/4'' (6.4mm). Each is specified for different activities. The size of the holes is not the same in both thicknesses, so you can't substitute one for the other.

The materials made from wood can be used unfinished, but a coat of clear spray finish will make them easy to clean. You can spray all of the boards at one time before cutting them.

Here are some other tips for buying supplies:

1. Golf tees—least expensive when bought in bulk at sporting goods stores. Check the length—1 7/8'' (4.8cm) is specified for all activities. Blunt the ends by rubbing them back and forth on sandpaper or rough concrete a few times, holding them straight up and down.
2. Key tags—sold in office supply stores by the hundred, which is approximately the number you need for all the exercises requiring them.
3. Tongue depressors—at your pharmacy. Unbelievably inexpensive. Ask for the wider kind, if you have a choice.
4. Clear plastic for laminating—get the heaviest available. Buy it by the yard at fabric stores and home centers.
5. Clear adhesive-backed plastic (Contact is one brand) for laminating—buy it by the yard in hardware stores and home centers.
6. Felt markers—buy only the permanent kind, not the water-based ones, which will smear with use. Marks-a-lot is a good brand. You'll need wide-tipped ones in four basic colors—red, blue, green and yellow plus black.
7. Food colors—most economical by the 1-oz (29.5ml) bottle; also in the four basic colors. Transfer them to small dropper bottles from a drugstore.
8. Glue—three kinds: white household glue, contact cement or epoxy glue. Although ordinary household white glue, such as Elmer's, will work in most instances, waterproof white glue is specified in some cases, and Wilhold is a good brand. In fact, it can be used anywhere Elmer's can. The new acrylic latex contact cements are convenient, but they won't bond some materials which the older kind will.
9. Velcro fastener—sold in fabric stores, by the inch.
10. Magnetic tape—sold in hobby stores, or handicraft stores, or check with a magnetic sign company. A wider width can be used in place of ½'' (12.7mm).
11. Nails—1'' (2.5cm) finishing nails are used throughout.
12. Felt—precut 9'' x 12'' (22.8cm x 30.5cm) rectangles are more convenient to use than felt by the yard. Most tabric and handicraft stores sell them. Iron-on interfacing (heavyweight) will make the felt much more wrinkle-proof; use it on all felt materials if you like.
13. Sponges—are of two types: cellulose and polyfoam. Both are specified. Don't substitute one kind for the other—they won't work. How to tell the difference: cellulose sponge labels usually say so and are packaged one to four to a package. Polyfoam sponges come in large bags of 12 or so.

Here are the tools you'll need:

1. Saw
2. Hammer
3. Ruler and yardstick
4. Paper stapler
5. Heavy-duty stapler, optional—hammer-in staples (hardware) can be used instead
6. Paper hole punch
7. Single-edge razor blade or X-acto knife
8. Scissors

Laminating

Pictures are more interesting encased in clear plastic than glued on cards, and simpler to do as well. Children come to look right through pictures after a while. They become commonplace. But pictures "floated" in plastic get attention! And they are practically indestructible. What more could we ask?

For laminating, use the clear plastic and adhesive-backed plastic described in TOOLS AND SUPPLIES. Keep it simple. Clear plastic is so forgiving, small discrepancies in measurement and unmatched edges will be unnoticed.

If the pictures you want to use have words or pictures on the back which would be confusing or distracting, cover them with black marker before laminating. Small pictures can be backed with a small square of paper, but it's not necessary.

The adhesive-backed plastic comes in 18'' (45.7cm) widths, and an 18'' (45.7cm) square is easy to work with, expecially if you have an extra pair of hands to help. It will make 36 3'' (7.6cm) squares; reduce the size to 9'' × 18'' (22.8cm × 45.7cm) or 9'' × 12'' (22.8cm × 30.5cm) if you're working alone. Here's how:

1. Use a ball point pen to measure a block the desired size on the clear plastic. No need to cut it out—it's easier to handle as part of a larger piece.
2. Use a yardstick and ball point pen to mark it into 3'' (7.6cm) squares. DON'T CUT YET.
3. Center pictures or the material to be laminated in the squares. *Put pictures face down.*
4. Cut a block of adhesive-backed plastic the same size as the block of clear plastic.
5. Peel the paper backing from it and lay it, adhesive side down, over the pictures, starting at the top edge and pressing as you move downward.
6. Cut the squares apart on the lines. Voila!

Suspension Rod

You'll love this little device. It provides a new perspective for viewing relationships. Relative sizes are easily seen in the vertical position, and necessary changes in arrangement are obvious. It is also an interesting change of pace: there is a certain satisfaction to suspending something in space.

The CYLINDERS exercise uses the SUSPENSION ROD, and it supports the BALANCE, the SCALE, and the PUPPET THEATRE. It is used in a doorway. Two sets of closet-pole sockets on either side of the doorway are permanently fixed, allowing quick positioning and removal of the Rod by students. One set is 28'' (71.1cm) from the floor; This is the height for all activities except the PUPPET THEATRE, which is used 38'' (96.5cm) from the floor; place the second set of sockets at this height. In a wooden door frame, attach the sockets with the screws provided in the package; in a metal door frame, use contact cement.

The rod itself is a wooden dowel ¾'' (19mm) diameter or larger, or you can use a closet pole if you happen to have one. Use a permanent marker to mark the center of the dowel. Make a dot 1 3/8'' (3.49cm) on either side of the center mark, and dots every 2 3/4'' (6.9cm) on either side of these, making 10 in all, 5 on each side of center. Put large screw eyes on the dots. Saw off the ends of the dowel to fit in the sockets in the doorway, sawing an equal amount off each end.

Remind your students that the SUSPENSION ROD is not a toy or exercise apparatus. It should be put in place just before use and removed immediately afterwards.

If you don't have a doorway which can be used for the SUSPENSION ROD, don't skip it! Put it between two cabinets, or on the back of one, or on a wall, with cafe curtain brackets. In these applications, it won't work for the PUPPET THEATRE, but it will work for the other activities.

Storage

Much of the success of an individualized program depends on appropriate storage. An exercise with missing parts is frustrating at the least, and in some cases totally useless. Shabby or flimsy containers devalue an activity and encourage its careless use. Fortunately, however, you can find satisfactory containers which cost little or nothing. Here are some ideas:

1. Trays—you can't have too many! They are invaluable for keeping organized. Local cafeterias and fast-food restaurants will usually donate or sell cheaply their chipped trays. Of course, you can buy them new from a restaurant supply.
2. Plastic containers—you can collect these as discards or buy them inexpensively. Plastic refrigerated food containers of different sizes are ideal if they are heavy enough to be reusable. Look for the ones whose printing is on removable labels. Printing on the container is unattractive. If you choose to buy containers, plastic freezer cartons and rattan plate holders are inexpensive. You won't need tops; they just get lost. Many fast-food restaurants buy some products in gallon or five-gallon plastic tubs and will usually save them for you if you ask. They make good storage containers for exercises with large parts. You will need a few rectangular plastic dishpans, but do shop around; prices vary a lot.

A Word About Safety

Wide-mouthed clear bottles or jars are used in several activities. For safety's sake, they should be of plastic, but obtaining them may be difficult. Glass baby food jars work perfectly, but do present problems with safety. The best source for plastic bottles is your pharmacist, who will probably be willing to order a box of them for you. They should be clear, not amber, hold 2 to 4 ounces (59 to 118ml) , (or more), and be wide mouthed. If caps are needed, get the screw-on or snap-on type, rather than the safety-lock type. If you can't get plastic bottles and decide to use baby food jars, keeping them in muffin tins minimizes the risk of breakage. They should be carried, used and stored in the muffin tins. If you do use baby food jars, put the caps (for those exercises requiring them) on newspaper and spray paint them to cover the writing.

Putting It In Their Hands

There are a few keys to maintaining a smoothly-run individualized program, and they should be adhered to consistently. Adults must:

1. Be sure demonstrations have preceded the use of each exercise.
2. Order the workshelves daily before the students arrive, or at the end of each school day.

Students, in turn, are responsible for:

1. Returning exercises to the workshelf in their storage containers.
2. Taking reasonable care to avoid damaging them during use.

While all the exercises have well-defined objectives, I'm not in favor of rigidly enforcing a prescribed manner of using them. Children may reach their own conclusions through their own unique approach to an exercise and these may be as valid as the intended ones. Surely, this golden age for discovery and exploration can best be served by encouraging the children's natural inclination to experiment. Most of the time they will attempt to duplicate as nearly as possible the teacher's pre-use demonstration; but not always! Be prepared for those original thinkers who have their own ideas about the objective of an exercise! Whether you interpret this as creative expression or misbehavior depends on many factors, and your response will vary accordingly. Though it is sometimes difficult to distinguish between puttering and purposeful activity, teachers usually know instinctively when students need to be admonished about the way they are using materials. Bear in mind that the indivdualized classroom is dynamic—it thrives on the unexpected. It is never static and predictable. In the end only you can decide what requires intervention and what can be ignored.

I believe students should be allowed to use an activity for as long or as short a time as they want; I also believe they shouldn't be required to complete an exercise before replacing it with another. Others may disagree; perhaps you consider finishing selected work a prime requisite. This is a matter of personal values. You should be aware, however, that such a rule may encourage children to repeat only the exercises they are sure they can complete and not venture to try new ones. Of course, a child who flits from one activity to another, rarely finishing one, is a distraction to others and must be helped to develop either more self-control or more maturity. You may have to suggest alternate (non-individualized) activities for him or her in the interim.

A hallmark of individualization is respect for a child's work as his or her own. Many teachers use praise to guarantee hard work and good performance. Others feel, as I do, that praise exacts a high toll in the end: it undermines confidence in oneself. When praise is not forthcoming, a child who has come to depend on it may be unable to function effectively. In my experience, success with individual exercises promotes a feeling of accomplishment and pride which makes praise superfluous. How, then, does an adult react to children's success with their work? A genuine expression of pleasure at their pleasure is just the right response.

There is also the related question of "checking" finished activities by an adult. Broadly speaking, I feel safe in relying on the positive forces which motivate children to do their best in order to satisfy their own needs. I do expect occasional lapses, though. (We adults don't perform at peak capacity a hundred percent of the time, either!) Again, you may disagree, feeling it is important to check finished work to correct mistakes, or you may feel checking is necessry to see that children don't concentrate on certain exercises to the exclusion of others. Both points are valid. One way to handle the latter problem is to keep written records of exercises performed, guiding children toward untried ones when the record shows it is indicated. This is especially true for kindergarten application. When the exercises augment a public school program, such as kindergarten, teachers may find it necessary to monitor their use more closely. At the preschool level, however, a loss of spontaneity is inevitable without a generous amount of flexibility. Think of the knowledge children accumulate before they enter school without the benefit of grades or marks. Remembering this helps me to relax and to trust the child's driving force which I mentioned earlier.

My experience has shown that there are three cardinal rules which can't be broken, or even bent, without seriously affecting your program. They are:

1. Activities should never be exchanged between students. They must always be replaced on the shelf before being taken by another person. (Otherwise, who is responsible for putting them away?)
2. Activities are used by one person at a time. Sharing individualized activities is not a good idea, though children may help each other. An activity can quickly become free-for-all play if several children work together. Play is wonderful, and shared play even more so, but not with an activity which requires the full concentration of the one in charge.
3. Parts from different exercises are never mixed while being used.

Play—or Work?

Individualized learning materials are not games; they don't need to be disguised to make them palatable, because they appeal to children's natural inquisitiveness. Toys and games belong in every child's life, but learning materials are not toys and even the youngest child knows this. It's best to call them what they are. And don't worry, children do not crave perpetual entertainment; they need extended opportunity for play, but they also have a need to test themselves occasionally.

The words "work" and "use" needn't be uncomfortable—they seem perfectly right after a while. "Do you want to use the CYLINDERS now?" and "You forgot to put away your work" are honest and direct. Be confident that your students are equal to these learning materials—and they will be.

Other Points to Remember

Having a vigorous, working individualized program is a joy, but it requires the discipline and vigilance of the entire staff. In particular, the workshelves *must* be checked daily. If more than one adult is present, a schedule of rotation for this duty is a good idea. Removing broken parts and recovering missing ones is extremely important. Children can't be expected to compensate for missing pieces. Counting, for instance, can be accurate only if all the things to be counted are there.

Inadequate work space will cause parts of different exercises to become mixed. Perhaps the best solution is small individual tables, but large tables work fine, too. If table space is inadequate, the logical move is to the floor. Some activities can be done better on the floor anyway. I strongly advise the use of mats, in most instances, instead of the bare floor, because mats contain the exercise parts and define the work space. They also prevent damage to materials from walkers-by. Remind children to walk around, not across, mats that are in use. You can buy mats made from carpet remnants at discount stores. Store them together and expect students to put away mats as well as materials after use.

An important question is what to do with exercises when they're not being used. This won't be a problem for preschools where children spend half a day. But in extended-day schools, where many hours are spent in free play and group activities, the exercises will be off-limits during these times. Because of the universal appeal of some items contained in the exercises, they may find their way into play if they're too accessible. How, without constant policing, to remedy this? Consider:

1. Slipping pieces of pegboard or hardboard on small nails or cup hooks on the edges of the shelves to cover the contents or
2. Draping a piece of fabric or a plastic paint drop cloth over the entire shelf unit.

First Come, First Served

Except for special cases, I believe this rule is a sound one to follow with individualized activities. Granted, new or especially popular activities may be overworked, but the situation is temporary, and, generally speaking, adult attempts at equitably matching activities and children compound the problem. It is important to recognize that children's development rarely follows a steady course. It moves in fits and starts. A child is insatiable for a certain activity for a time; this is followed by an almost latent period—a rest, so it seems—then he or she plunges headlong into a new interest, and the cycle is repeated.

Repetition of activities—all activities—is to be encouraged, not discouraged by requiring "taking turns." Fair play is expected, of course, but unless overtly aggressive behavior is involved, it's acceptable for a child to choose the same activity daily for a while, even a new activity, and to use it for as long as he wishes. After all, there are many things others can do in the meantime, and it will all even out in the end. It's usually not worthy of adult intervention. This sort of social by-play is what school is all about and is best handled by the ones directly involved: the students. If adult monitoring is not forthcoming, they will do a surprisingly good job of monitoring themselves.

But Who Cleans Up?

The use of individualized materials implies responsibility for cleaning up after oneself. When a child consistently ignores cleanup, your only alternative is to temporarily deny him or her use of individualized materials. This is fair. Find other activities and let him or her try again soon. You'll be surprised at how infrequently this happens. Children have greater control of their own behavior in the individualized classroom, and in turn they're willing to assume greater responsiblity. Within a short time, they accept clean-up as the last step in any exercise.

Please don't avoid some of the exercises because they are "messy" in favor of "clean" ones! You'll miss so much if you do! Learning is sometimes messy. The exercises that use water, paint, etc. add something invaluable. You may have to raise the responsibility quotient of the class, but that's easy—you simply give them more to be responsible for! Never underestimate the power of the positive: the expectation to behave responsibly is self-fulfilling. Forget conventional attitudes about messiness—unafraid teachers frequently have to disregard convention and set new boundaries. You'll be glad you did!

Clean-up

In most instances, clean-up consists of putting the materials back in the containers and the containers back on the shelf. With activities using water, sand, rice, etc. some minor spilling is inevitable. It's cleaned by the child who used the activity, with child-sized equipment. The broom or whiskbroom and dustpan will clean rice on the floor (throw it away, don't replace it in the container), the mop is needed for splashed water, and tables are dried with a towel for the next user, to prevent damage to materials. Spilled paint or food color will usually yield to baking soda scrubbing.

Don't be concerned that children feel resentful of being expected to clean their own spills—they don't. They will even scrub tables that are clean and mop spotless floors. That's O.K., too, because clean-up can stand on its own as a developmental activity. For eye-hand coordination and control of materials, it's par excellence. It doubles the learning value of an exercise. Demonstrate the use of each piece of cleaning equipment, emphasizing such points as the need to squeeze excess water from sponges and the mop, and the use of the broom, whiskbroom and dustpan. Do provide both a broom and whiskbroom; the broom is for collecting spilled sand, rice, etc., and the whiskbroom can be used to push it into the dustpan without a second person holding it.

Clean-Up Supplies

These should be included in the LIFE ARTS section of the classroom. Put the hanging things on hooks on the ends of shelf units or on the wall, and place the others on the shelf.

1. A child's broom
2. A child's mop
3. A small pail for mopping
4. A toy dustpan
5. A whiskbroom
6. Sponges—for cleaning tables only—never floors, to prevent spread of germs
7. Towels—4 to 6—small dishtowels are best; they may be cut in half
8. A small basket or hamper for used towels
9. A small drying rack for towels—either a folding rack or a clothesline strung between two points
10. Unbreakable shaker such as a salt shaker, for baking soda to use as a cleanser. It's non-toxic and cleans quite well. A small amount at a time in the shaker will prevent over-zealousness by the user.
11. 2 plastic pitchers—one which holds 1½ or 2 qts (1.4 liters or 1.89 liters) and a small one holding a pint (473ml), such as a 2-cup measuring cup. Make a fill mark on each at 2/3 full with a permanent marker.

Making It All Work

Age Grouping

With my own classes, I've found these activities suited to 2 to 6 year-olds. I have indicated the level of difficulty for each exercise by defining "Beginners" as 2 and 3 year-olds, "Intermediate" as 4 year-olds and "Advanced" as 5 years and beyond.

Some students benefit by working with exercises below their own age level; this builds their confidence to attempt more advanced ones. Such children need to take life in manageable portions, and small successes are crucial for them.

Two-to-three year olds need more direct guidance than older children as they learn to work independently; I have suggestions for this in A NOTE ABOUT BEGINNERS.

Regard the above ages as guidelines only—if you feel a particular exercise is right for your class, it probably is. Only you know the special needs and strengths of your students. Don't hesitate to challenge their reach; on the other hand, repeated frustration from attempting too-difficult exercises is certainly to be avoided. Try to achieve a stituation in which most of the students can experience success with most of the exercises. A broad mix with some above and some below the actual age level of the class seems to work best.

Sometimes individualized classes are vertically grouped; that is, children of different but compatible ages and stages of development are grouped together. Usually, a feeling of community develops as a consequence of the interaction between these children. Older children can be seen helping younger ones, reinforcing their own skills in the process. An atmosphere of easy give-and-take prevails. If this appeals to you, you may want to give vertical grouping a try. Just be sure that the level of activities exceeds the ability of the oldest children to assure their maximum growth.

Vertical grouping is by no means the only way to use these individualized exercises. They are just as effective in traditionally age-grouped classes. Use them as you would any other single-student materials. More about this in the section AN OVERVIEW OF THE INDIVIDUALIZED CLASSROOM.

Vocabulary Enrichment

An individualized learning program creates natural communication between teacher and student. If language development is a primary objective, talking about, in addition to working with, the materials can be made part of the program. One way to approach this is to coordinate individualized work with group lessons and experiences. Some activities will correlate with units of study on almost any subject. Introduction of the exercises can be timed to coincide with units throughout the year, and they can then remain a part of class activities if desired. Field trips and excursions can lead into selected follow-up exercises, as well.

Ways of introducing word usage with exercises can be as varied and as spontaneous as classroom situations suggest. Countless opportunities for conversation between adults and children will present themselves. This begins, of course, with the pre-use demonstration given by the teacher in which he names the parts of the exercise, describes their functions, and invites discussion to clarify understanding of their use.

The most fruitful conversational exchanges between adults and children are possible in schools blessed with volunteer help, because of the high staff-pupil ratio. Parent cooperatives are one example. During one-to-one exchanges an easy flow of talk occurs naturally. Remember to listen at least as much as you talk—otherwise you may find yourself in a "star" role again! All teachers are super elicitors—leading comments can go far to encourage even the most reticent student.

If you are the only adult in your classroom, circulating among the busy children will automatically generate a certain amount of discussion, and this can be used to advantage. However, be alert to the temptation to interfere, unless intervention is clearly indicated or help is requested. Solving minor dilemmas for oneself is an important part of an individualized program and the worker's attempts in that direction must be respected. As a general rule, if a child is struggling but has not asked for help, and seems to be moving in the right direction, no help is indicated. Conversely, intervention is needed in cases of misuse of materials or if the student is obviously so confused that a successful outcome is impossible. An individual repeat demonstration of the exercise is probably needed in both instances.

As to literal help with an exercise, I have always felt it's wise for adults to maintain a "hands-off" policy for the most part. It's so tempting to quickly rearrange the offending pieces of an exercise for a student who is at an impasse. Don't! Not even if he asks you to. A quick assessment of the situation and a few minutes spent showing interest, defining the problem, and perhaps questions about his actions to this point will usually set things aright and you and he can move on. Your genuine concern, and the support lent by your presence, may be all that is needed.

Overview of Individualization in Practice

I'm going to try to paint a picture of an individualized classroom for you. If you stepped inside one, here is what you might see:

Children would be using materials from all the centers. Learning is learning; art or numbers, woodworking or puzzles; it can all happen comfortably at the same time in the same place.

After staff members have directed the class to find work, and helped those who seem uncertain to make selections, they move around the room among the students at the tables, and on the floor. You might be surprised to hear only children's voices. The adults are busy observing and helping, but they seem to have a special radar that picks up on things even several feet away. They seem to know intuitively when an exercise has been abandoned carelessly on a mat or table. Someone goes directly to the student and reminds her that her work has not been put away.

Everything is running smoothly for the most part—there's an almost perceptible hum about the room. As always, a busy group is at work in Construction—funny, the same ones seem to inhabit that section day after day, while others rarely do. Teachers seem to feel that a balance will eventually be reached and they make little effort to direct the children in their choices. One adult is checking a clip-board, apparently to help a student who has been unsettled up to now to find work; then she sits down with him to help him get started.

One thing strikes you as different from other classrooms: though the children are working independently, there seems to be a lot of child-helping-child, too. When no adult is free to help or to answer a question, they seem automatically to turn to each other, and help is rarely refused. You remember hearing a teacher say that the emphasis is on cooperation, not competition. Children really do help each other, as well as themselves. The child who has been examining rocks with a magnifying glass has spent the entire morning in the same spot, seemingly oblivious to everything around her, while another has had only the briefest contact with several activities. But overall, most of the students have seemed absorbed in their work and have paced themselves well.

When a teacher taps on a hand bell, signalling the end of the session, there is a general unhurried scurrying about, and materials are put back in their places. One thing about this last scene catches your eye—few children rush to put away their work as though they're anxious to escape it, and a few cling to what they're doing until they're reminded that they can use the same activity again tomorrow.

Pre-use Demonstrations

How did the class you just saw learn to use the materials so that they could work with so little adult direction? The secret was in pre-use demonstrations and individual lessons, important groundwork you missed. The activities had been introduced one at a time, and most had also had a follow-up individual lesson before each child used it for the first time. It was a slow start, admittedly; the materials were introduced no closer together than one every three days, and children who hadn't had lessons sometimes had to wait until an adult was free to give one. But the time and work required by demonstrations and individual lessons was well spent. They made the smooth operation you witnessed possible.

The pre-use demonstration should pique the child's interest, but not exhaust the activity's possibilities. In other words, aim at providing just enough direction to assure that the activity will be used in a way that maximizes its potential without limiting its options. Raise questions and leave answers to be discovered. "What if?" has a delicious expectancy about it.

Do be specific on two points: 1. each and every step used to carry out the activity, including bringing water to the workspace if it's needed, putting the parts back in the storage container with care, and each step of appropriate cleanup, and 2. vocabulary—expand this to the fullest: name parts, invite discussion and questions. But appreciate the delicacy of this operation. Using words which are far beyond the children's comprehension is both useless and harmful. Parroting meaningless (to them) words is not in learning's best interest. Children's development is a fragile thing, happening in its own time. We enrich it by widening their acquaintance with words which can become a permanent part of their vocabulary. The most valuable thing we can do is to help them express what they already know. We don't want to complicate their speech, which is difficult enough already.

Take your time when giving a demonstration; this is a unique opportunity for teacher-student communication—make the most of it. Try to be the center of a small group of children; if you must show an entire class at one time, compensate by going slowly and repeating.

A good demonstration is like the presentation of a gift, with you as the giver and the students as the recipients. It is not an assignment. If you let your own enthusiasm for the new activity show, they will receive it in the same spirit. Make it an occasion!

Some activites won't require individual lessons. If, in your opinion, one can be used without them, make this clear in the pre-use demonstration. Otherwise, emphasize the need to ask for a lesson before using it. Whether or not an activity requires individual lessons depends somewhat on the class; each teacher must decide on the basis of her knowledge of the class. If in doubt, give lessons.

Individual Lessons

In an individual lesson, let the student be in charge of the activity. Observe to be sure he or she is using the materials correctly and understands the objective. "Will you show me what you know about this?" is a good way to begin. This is in no way a test of the student's knowledge or skills, but an offer of help, if it's needed. Move on as soon as you're not needed, but not before. It may be necessary to interrupt the activity if the child's understanding of an exercise is obviously confused. Repeat the pre-use demonstration. You may choose to keep a record of individual lessons given. If you do, a clipboard chart on the wall in a central location is a help—all staff members can check off lessons as they are given. This is also a record showing which students need to be directed toward untried exercises.

A Note About Beginners

Alas, fewer activities in this book are geared for 2–3 year-olds than for other ages. I wish it weren't so; there is a dearth of material for that age group. On the positive side, though, you can adapt some activities which are specified for Intermediates and Advanced to use with Beginners. Innovate, Experiment. In determining the age levels for a particular exercise, several questions must be considered. For example, how many 2–3 year-olds is one adult responsible for, not only in terms of teaching but in terms of safety? Many exercises which are not suitable for Beginners with casual adult supervision are suitable with an unusually favorable teacher-pupil ratio and close supervision. A one-to-one arrangement opens even more doors; the range is widened if an adult can work with three to four children at a time. So, examine each activity as it relates to your Beginners, and modify it as inspiration dictates.

Storing individualized materials on open shelves is not a good idea with young Beginners—those under three. Bring the materials to them for individualized sessions. Three-year-olds can usually manage choosing and returning activities on their own with some reminding and assistance.

Discrimination

Young children often show a surprising resistance to change. Their insistence that things stay *the way they are* reflects their need for predictability and consistency. Did you ever notice they don't really like surprises? They take comfort in returning things to the way they were; they're reassured by making parts whole again.

DISCRIMINATION exercises capitalize on this need to "make things make sense." They invite sorting, grading, ordering and matching—systematizing disorder—and children happily rise to the occasion.

Color Sticks

Level:
  Beginning-Intermediate

Objective:
  To match sticks which have the same color combinations.

Skills:
  Visual discrimination, matching

Vocabulary:
  Names of colors

Materials:
  • 16–24 tongue depressors for 8–12 pairs

  • Colored permanent markers—red, yellow, green, blue, black; others optional

  • Storage container

Construction:
  Color only one side of the sticks. Color each half a different color and make two of each combination. Make a black line across the center where the two colors meet.

Procedure:
  Put the sticks on the worksurface in random order. Match pairs by stacking them together. Repeat as desired.

Magnet Sort

Level:
Beginning to Advanced

Objective:
To sort the magnets by attaching them to the metal cookie sheet.

Skills:
Sorting, observation of magnetism, organizing

Vocabulary:
Magnet, row, sort, names of the novelty items on the magnets

Materials:
- 5 identical sets of novelty magnets
- Non-aluminum cookie sheet
- Storage container

Construction:
None required.

Procedure:
A cookie sheet is needed for several exercises which use magnets or magnetic tape. One cookie sheet can be used for all of them.

In this exercise, the magnets are sorted by rows, either vertically or horizontally, as they are placed on the sheet. They may also be grouped, likes together, or sets together—experimentation is encouraged.

Sandpaper Sticks

Level:
Intermediate-Advanced

Objective:
To match 6 sticks of like-textured sandpaper by feel.

Skills:
Tactile discrimination, concentration

Vocabulary:
Sandpaper, rough, smooth

Materials:
- 12 tongue depressors
- Sandpaper in coarse and fine textures
- White glue
- Storage container

Construction:
Cut 6 strips of each grade of sandpaper, 5/8'' (16mm) wide and 5'' (127mm) long. Brush glue generously on the sticks, all the way to both side edges and to within 1/4'' (6mm) of the ends. Center the sandpaper strips and press firmly. Blot by pressing on a paper towel. Be sure all edges are glued securely. Weight down overnight if necessary.

Procedure:
Place sticks in random order on the worksurface. By feeling the sticks, find the 6 of each grade and stack them. Children may close their eyes to feel the sticks or keep them open. Both grades of sandpaper should be the same color to eliminate matching by sight.

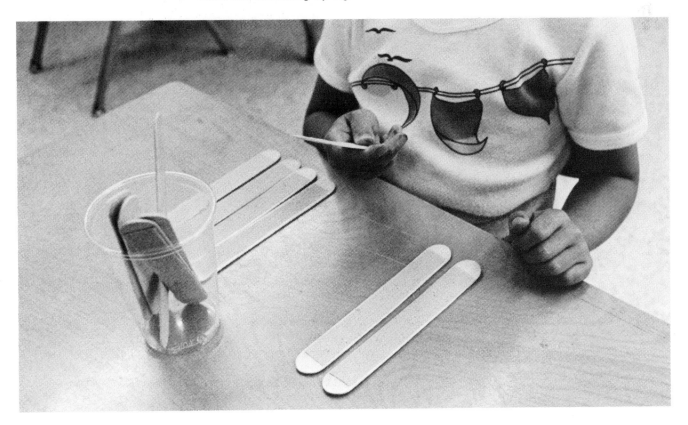

Cylinders

Objective:
To complete the dowel cylinders by finding pieces of the same diameter; ordering them from small to large on the SUSPENSION ROD.

Skills:
Size discrimination, observation of graduation, making comparisons, manual dexterity

Vocabulary:
Cylinder, connect, hook

Materials:
- 6 or more wooden dowels, ranging in diameter from 1/4'' (6mm) diameter upward
- 18 small (1/2'' [12.7mm]) cup hooks
- Storage container

Construction:
Cut the dowels in half or have them cut where you buy them. Use one set of the halves for this exercise and save the other set for RODS. For CYLINDERS, cut one set of the half-dowels into half again. Put cup hooks on both ends of half of them and on only one end of the other half.

Procedure:
The exercise may be done two ways: 1. match diameters first and connect the cylinders. Then find the smallest in diameter and hang it on the SUSPENSION ROD, and proceed to the next smallest. Or, 2. hang the pieces with hooks on both ends on the ROD in correct order and then add the matching pieces. Remove the cylinders and repeat in the reverse order, beginning with the largest, as an option.

Washer Bar

Level:

Beginning to Advanced

Objective:

To sort and grade the washers according to size as you place them on the board.

Skills:

Manual dexterity, comparing, grading

Vocabulary:

Washers

Materials:

- A piece of 1'' × 2'' (2.5cm × 5cm) board, 12'' (30.5cm) long
- 5 small finishing nails
- 25 washers; five sets of five each in graduated sizes
- Storage container

Construction:

Make a light pencil line down the lengthwise center of the board and space the nails every 2'' (5cm) along the line.

Procedure:

Teach two ways of ordering the washers and encourage students to do the two exercises in sequence; or they can do only one if they want. SORTING: stack all of the smallest size washers on the first nail, the next smallest ones on the second nail and so on. GRADING: stack graduated towers on the nails, with the largest washers on the bottom, up to the smallest on top, making five identical towers.

Patterns

Level:
Beginning to Advanced

Objective:
Beginners: to put the poker chips on the outlines on the mats.

Intermediate: to duplicate the patterns by placing the poker chips on the blank sides of the mats.

Advanced: to duplicate the patterns *and* stack the specified number of chips on the outlines.

Skills:
Visual perception, attention to detail, placement awareness, counting (Advanced)

Vocabulary:
Chips, pattern, corner, center, top, bottom, side

Materials:
- Beginners: 2 light-colored felt rectangles, 9" x 12" (23cm x 30cm)
  Intermediate and Advanced: 4 felt rectangles 9" x 12" (23cm x 30cm)
- Beginners and Intermediate: 24 poker chips; Advanced see below.
- Wide black marker
- 2 storage containers

Construction:
For all levels: cut mats in half crosswise, making two 6" x 9" (15cm x 23cm) pieces from each.

For Beginners: Cut the four mats in half again, making 8 pieces, each 4½" x 6" (11cm x 15cm). Trace around one poker chip in all the positions on the mats.

For Intermediates: Use the mats 6" × 9" (15cm × 23cm). Each one will have outlines on one half, a blank on the other half for duplicating the pattern. Draw a line down the crosswise center of each mat with the marker. Trace around a poker chip to produce the patterns on one half of each mat.

For Advanced: Make mats as for Intermediates. Use the marker to make from 1 to 10 dots in each of the outlines, in random order.

Patterns:
Mat #1: 1 circle in any position on the mat
    2: 2 circles diagonally
    3: 2 circles side by side
    4: 3 circles diagonally
    5: 3 circles triangularly
    6: 4 circles, one in each corner
    7: 4 cirlces, one on each side
    8: 5 circles, one in each corner, one in the middle

Procedure:

Beginners: place the mats on the worksurface. Place the poker chips, one by one, on the outlines on the mats.

Intermediate: place mats in rows of 2 or 4 on the worksurface. Duplicate the patterns on the mats by placing poker chips in the same positions on the blank halves.

Advanced: place mats in rows of 2 or 4. The number specified by the dots in the outlines must be stacked in the same position on the blank side of the mat.

Provide a container large enough for the mats to be stored flat, and a smaller one for the chips. Caution students to put the mats in first, then the container of chips, to avoid wrinkling the mats.

Sensory Bottles

Level:
  Beginning to Advanced
  (Beginning with adult
  assistance)

Objective:
  To pair the matching bottles by sound, smell, weight or temperature.

Skills:
  Sound distinction, olfactory perception, baric sense, temperature distinction

Vocabulary:
  Heavy, light, warm, cool, names of aromatics, descriptions of sounds

Materials:
  • Frozen juice cans, large size, (with snap-on lids)—8 for each set

  • SOUND BOTTLES—salt, 2 pennies, 2 paper clips, rice

  • AROMA BOTTLES—cinnamon, vanilla, peppermint or other flavoring, ginger or nutmeg

  • BARIC BOTTLES—sand or salt

  • THERMAL BOTTLES—no ingredients needed

  • 4 felt rectangles, 9" × 12" (23cm × 30cm)

- Contact paper (adhesive backed plastic)—see CONSTRUCTION notes below.
- Cotton balls
- Contact cement or epoxy
- 4 storage containers

Construction:

Each set of 8 bottles has 2 different colors or patterns—make 4 of each. Each set must have different colors and/or patterns from the others. For SOUND BOTTLES, put some of each shaking material in each pair. For AROMA BOTTLES, put the flavorings on cotton balls for each pair and put a drop of glue in the bottoms of the cans to hold the balls in place. For BARIC BOTTLES, fill the pairs from empty to full, increasing by thirds with salt or sand. Put contact cement or epoxy around the entire top edge of SOUND and BARIC BOTTLES only and press lids on firmly. Snap lids on and off AROMA BOTTLES for use. THERMAL BOTTLES don't use lids.

For sorting mats, use a wide marker to mark around one of the bottles 8 times on each mat, as shown.

Procedure:

SENSORY BOTTLES are so rich with skill-development potential, they're really worth the time it takes to make all four sets. They'll become classroom basics. Plan to spend plenty of time teaching the correct way to use them. Their value as learning tools depends to a large extent on the way they are used, because children must know how to keep them paired and organized during use. If tried and untried bottles become mixed, the exercise disintegrates into a guessing game, not at all the objective.

Each set is a separate exercise and they should be used one set at a time, never combined. The four sets may be used in succession, of course. Each set is used the same way. As an example, here is how to use SOUND BOTTLES:
1. separate the four bottles of each color or pattern in rows. Pick up a bottle of one row in one hand, one of the other row in the other hand. Shake them, separately and together, close to your ears and listen carefully, several times.
2. If they sound alike, place them together on the sorting mat. If they don't, keep one of them and put the other back, trying another of the same color or pattern.

Stress the importance of having one of each pattern or color in each hand. Continue until all are paired on the sorting mat. Notice the AROMA BOTTLES' lids snap on and off—they're not glued on.

THERMAL BOTTLES are an occasional-use exercise, prepared by an adult. Put the bottles empty on the shelf. They must be used soon after preparation before the temperatures change. Put water of four distinct temperatures from very cold to very warm in the bottles. Pair by feeling the outsides.

Storage containers should allow the bottles to stand vertically—clear plastic shoe boxes work perfectly. Store mats underneath.

Pos/Neg Viewers

Level:
Beginning to Advanced

Objective:
To find the positive and negative of each pair of transparent designs by superimposing them.

Skills:
Visual discrimination, logic, abstraction

Vocabulary:
Match, whole, part, complete

Materials:

- Heavyweight clear plastic (see LAMINATING, in PUTTING IT ALL TOGETHER)
- Clear adhesive-backed plastic
- Permanent colored markers
- 16 tongue depressors
- Paper stapler
- Container for storage

Construction:

Make 8 paper patterns, each 3½'' × 5½'' (8.9cm × 14cm), of these designs, or your own, using a ruler: diamond, triangle, circle, checkerboard, thirds crosswise, halves diagonally (corner to corner), fourths corner to corner, and fourths vertically. Use a ball point pen and yardstick to mark a 14'' × 22'' (35.5cm × 55.9cm) rectangle on the plastic. Divide it into 16 rectangles, four across, four down, making each one 5½'' × 3½'' (14cm × 8.9cm). DON'T CUT YET. Slip one of the paper patterns under the first rectangle and use a marker to make a positive of the design in one color; change colors and move the pattern to the next rectangle to make its negative. Use long downward strokes, rather than back-and -forth or up-down ones. Continue with all the patterns. Cut a piece of adhesive-backed plastic 15'' × 23'' (38cm × 58.4cm) (allowing an extra inch (2.5cm), peel off the paper backing and place it over the rectangles, beginning at the top and pressing downward. Cut out the rectangles. Staple a tongue depressor to the back of each one, centering it lengthwise, using 4 staples—2 at the top, 2 at the bottom.

Note: It is helpful to have four hands to lay the piece of adhesive-backed plastic. If an extra pair are not available, you may want to cut the colored rectangles apart and lay them inked side down on the adhesive, then trim to fit.

Procedure:

Spread all the viewers on the worksurface in random order. Find matches by holding them up, one in front of the other, to the light. Stack matches together.

Sorting Bar

Level:
Beginning to Advanced

Objective:
To put the key tags on the nails on the bar in several sorting and matching exercises.

Skills:
One-to-one correspondence, sorting, categorizing

Vocabulary:
Words which relate to the pictures chosen.

Materials:

- Key tags, 1¼'' (32mm) diameter—office supply
- Adhesive picture seals—teachers supply, stationery stores
- Permanent colored markers
- Two 18'' (45cm) long 1'' × 2'' (2.5cm × 5cm) boards
- 16 small finishing nails
- 3 storage containers

Construction:

Make a light pencil line down the center lengthwise of the boards and space 8 nails on each, 2'' (5cm) from the ends and between nails.

FOR COLOR SORT —use the colored markers to color one side of 24 tags. Use red, yellow, blue and green, plus combinations of each color and black, coloring one half of the key tags with each of the colors, and the other half black. Or use purple, orange, brown and black if they are available and omit the combinations. Make three of each color and of each combination.

For PICTURE SORT—stick 8 different picture seals on key tags; make 3 of each, 24 in all.

For CLASSIFYING—stick 8 different pictures of each category—plants, animals, etc. on key tags, making 1 set of each. Each set will have 16 tags; e.g., 8 plants, 8 animals.

Procedure:

The sorting/matching exercises should be used singly to avoid mixing them. Using them in sequence is a good idea. Store each set in its own container. Rotate them if mixed sets become a problem. If you can't find 8 of each thing specified, use fewer and put the corresponding number of nails on the boards.

The three exercises are:

1. COLOR SORT—three tags of each color are stacked on a single nail using one board.
2. PICTURE SORT—uses picture seals of trees, flowers, animals, etc.—three alike are stacked on the nails on one board.
3. CLASSIFYING—uses 2 boards—2 different categories of picture seals are classified by placing them on separate boards—animals/plants, people/toys, etc.

Trinket Lotto

Level:
Intermediate-Advanced

Objective:
To play a cooperating game with a partner and a caller—to match real objects with their outlines on felt playing mats.

Skills:
Visual distinction, abstraction, focus on detail, cooperation

Vocabulary:
Caller, names of all the trinkets used

Materials:
- A 9''×12'' (23cm×30cm) light-colored felt rectangle, cut in half, or two 6''×9'' (15cm×23cm) pieces
- Black marker
- 12 different trinkets such as a thimble, ring, guitar pick, costume jewelry stones, dice, tiny artificial flower, birthday candle, tiny car, little birthday favor-type trinkets, etc.
- Two storage containers

Construction:
Mark the playing mats into 6 squares with the marker and a ruler, by making a line halfway across (lengthwise) and two lines up and down, 3'' (8cm) apart (crosswise). Trace around the trinkets on the squares, one trinket per square.

Procedure:

This game is for two players plus a caller. The person choosing it asks one child to be her partner (not competitor—there is no winner or loser), and another child to be the caller. Each of the two partners has a playing mat and the caller has the container of trinkets, which he holds up one at a time for the players to see. The player whose mat contains an outline of the object takes it and places it on the outline. When both players' mats are filled, the players exchange mats, or the caller may change places with a player and the game is repeated if all agree. The one whose mat is filled first is not the "winner"—there is no winner. Competition is discouraged by emphasizing the partner relationship. For obvious reasons, the container of trinkets may need to be stored separately; the mats can stay on the shelf. Students may ask an adult for them and return them at the end of the game. The game may be extended to 3 or 4 players if enough trinkets can be found. The container for the mats must be large enough to allow them to lie flat to avoid wrinkling. Put the container of trinkets on top of the mats if they are stored together.

Large/Small Stamps

Level:

Intermediate-Advanced

Objective:

To use corks as stamps on paper, matching large and small sizes and ordering them from large to small.

Skills:

Visual perception, manual dexterity, grading, ordering

Vocabulary:

Stamp, cork

Materials:

- Corks in graduated sizes (look for a bag of assorted sizes—housewares departments or supermarkets)

- Paper

- Food color

- Stamp pad

- Storage container

Construction:

None required.

Procedure:

Note: A stamp pad is used for several different activities, and a single one can be used for all. Buy an uninked pad. "Ink" will be food color. Put several drops of full-strength food color on the pad, and then a tablespoon (15ml) or so of clear water. Press in several places with one of the stamps to make the pad absorb the water. Hereafter when the pad is used, simply add clear water (a plastic squeeze bottle is handy). Add more food color when the prints become too light.

Long, narrow strips of paper approximately 10'' × 3'' (25cm × 8cm), or cash register tape, work best with this exercise. Put a supply of such strips with it if you want to save larger sheets of paper for activities which require them.

Begin the exercise with experimentation. Use the stamps to make random prints on a strip of paper, then order the corks from large to small (or reversed) on the worksurface before beginning again. Turn the paper over and stamp, beginning with the largest cork and ending with the smallest, (or reverse) or stamp with the large end and then the small end beside it. Do as many sets as desired, unless paper is limited. Put finished work in personal storage spaces.

Pos/Neg Stamps

Level:
Intermediate-Advanced

Objective:
To find the corresponding positive and negative of each design; to stamp them on paper.

Skills:
Abstraction, visualization, logic

Vocabulary:
Stamps, matching, pair

Materials:
- 4 rectangular erasers (not gum)
- X-acto knife or single-edge razor blade
- Paper

- Food color
- Stamp pad
- Tray or storage container

Construction:
Cut the erasers in half crosswise. Use the designs shown or your own, but keep them simple, to facilitate carving. Cut each one approximately 1/8" (3mm) deep, making a positive and a negative for four different designs.

Procedure:
Prepare the stamp pad as described under LARGE/SMALL STAMPS. Small pieces of paper work best with the exercise; it's a good idea to put a supply with it.

Begin the exercise with experimentation. Stamp for enjoyment and discovery. Then turn the paper over and try one or several matching exercises: superimpose each "positive" with its "negative" (or vice versa) to prove the matches, or stamp matched pairs side by side, or any other way that appeals. Put finished work in personal storage spaces.

Color Bottles

Level:
Intermediate-Advanced

Objective:
To grade the bottles of colored water from light to dark.

Skills:
Discernment, attention to detail, visual distinction, color recognition

Vocabulary:
Lightest, darkest, light, dark, medium, color names

Materials:
- 12 small clear plastic bottles and caps
- Food colors—red, blue, yellow, green
- Contact cement or epoxy glue
- Storage container

Construction:
In order to achieve the lightest shade of each color, it's necessary to use a full cup of water, and add one drop of food color. Mix in a measuring cup and fill the bottle with the solution. For the medium and dark shades, fill the bottles with water. Add one drop of color to make the medium shades and three drops to make the dark shades. Attach the lids on permanently with contact cement or epoxy glue.

Procedure:

Sort the bottles by color families first—put all the red family together, all the green family, etc. Then put the darkest of one color on the bottom, stack the medium shade on top of that, and the lightest shade on top of that. Repeat for all 4 colors. Repeat, reversing the order, going from light to dark. (Either order may be used first.) Place the colors in rows of three, too—experiment. The container should allow the bottles to stand.

Note: If children have trouble distinguishing the 3 shades, suggest they hold a white sheet of paper behind the bottles, or hold them up to a light source.

Magnet Strips

Level:

Intermediate-Advanced

Objective:

To attach the magnetic strips on the cookie sheet in several variations.

Skills:

Appreciation of magnetism, graduation, organization, postive-negative

Vocabulary:

Strips, magnet, stairs, pyramid

Materials:

- 2 rolls (60'' [152cm] each) of magnetic tape, ½'' (13mm) wide—hobby or handicraft stores

- Non-aluminum cookie sheet

- Plastic tape—2 colors, ¾'' (19mm) wide

- Storage container

Construction:

Lay the magnetic tape on the cookie sheet for easy handling while applying the colored tape. Peel the paper from the magnetic tape and apply one color of the plastic tape on the adhesive side even with one edge, extending over the other edge. Press firmly and trim the excess. Cut 10 pieces with scissors, beginning with 1'' (25mm) and increasing each piece by 1'' (25mm). Fifty-five inches are used; five inches of each roll will not be used. Repeat for second color.

Procedure:

Encourage students to experiment with different arrangements of the strips. Try these three, plus any others you or they think of: (place the cookie sheet horizontally for all three.)

1. Positive/Negative—Place the shortest bar of one color horizontally and build to the longest, keeping the edge even. Add the second colored set at the ends of the first bars, in reverse order—the longest at the end of the shortest, etc.

2. Stairs—place the bars vertically—all of one color, beginning on the outside with the shortest piece. At the center, reverse the stairs, going down, with the second color.

3. Pyramid—place the longest bar horizontally and go to the shortest on top, centering one above the other. Use the second color to build a second pyramid upside down on the first.

If space permits, leave 1/4''–3/8'' (6mm–10mm) space between the strips in all arrangements.

Rings

Level:
Beginning-Intermediate

Objective:
To order the rings according to size; to fit them inside one another concentrically.

Skills:
Size discrimination, visual discrimination, ordering

Vocabulary:
Ring, order, fit

Materials:
- 6 to 8 metal, plastic or wood macrame rings in graduated sizes—handicraft and hobby stores
- Long metal bolt
- Heavy cord

- 12–16 small S-hooks
- Storage container

Construction:

To make the Hanging Cords, cut a 12'' (30cm) length of cord for each ring. Tie S-hooks on both ends and use pliers to bend one end of the hooks to close over the cord to prevent it from slipping off.

Procedure:

Find the smallest ring, then the next smallest, up to the largest and order them in a horizontal line on the worksurface. Reverse the order and start with the largest. Try vertical rows both ways. Fit them together concentrically: place the largest one on the surface, then the next largest inside that, etc. to the smallest. Start with the smallest and reverse the order. The activity can consist of all or any part of these variations—enjoy. To make MUSICAL RINGS, (metal rings only) attach the Hanging Cords and suspend from the SUSPENSION ROD (see SUSPENSION ROD in PUTTING IT ALL TOGETHER. Strike on the inside with the bolt.

Puzzle Sticks

Level:

Beginning to Advanced

Objective:

To complete the picture by placing the sticks side by side.

Skills:

Deduction, visual distinction, follow through

Vocabulary:

Conversational exchange pertinent to the activity

Materials:

- 8 tongue depressors for each puzzle
- Colored permanent markers
- Tape
- Storage containers

Construction:

Use two strips of tape to tape 8 sticks together on the back side to hold them together while you work. On the top side, draw the design in pencil and fill in with the colored markers. Part of the design must be on each stick. Outline the picture with the wide point of the black marker. Remove the tape strips.

Procedure:

If you're lucky, as I was, and know someone who is artistic, these little puzzles are a snap. If not, don't despair—just copy pictures from children's workbooks or enlarge cookie cutter designs. To make reversible puzzles, put a design on both sides. Make as many as you like. To do the puzzles simply put them together to complete the pictures. For Beginners, make each puzzle a separate exercise and substitute geometric shapes for pictures. For Intermediates and Advanced, you may choose to group all the puzzles as one exercise. If you do, provide a separate container for each, but put all the containers on a tray or in a larger container.

Note: Choose bold, simple designs. To raise the level of difficulty, make the design more elaborate or use more sticks.

Pattern Sticks

Level:
Beginning to Advanced

Objective:
To find pairs of like patterns of fabric or wallpaper which will fit together to complete the pattern.

Skills:
Visual distinction, matching

Vocabulary:
Dots, stripes, plaid, etc.

Materials:
- 12 different fabric or wallpaper samples (discontinued upholstery or wallpaper books)
- 24 tongue depressors
- White glue
- Storage container

Construction:
Cut a strip of wallpaper or fabric 1¼'' (32mm) wide and 5'' (127mm) long for each pair. Cut it in half lengthwise to make 2 strips (5/8'' [16mm] wide each) which will match when placed side by side. Use pinking shears with fabric, if possible. Brush glue on the sticks all the way to the side edges and to within ¼'' (6mm) of the ends. Center the strips and press firmly. Press on a paper towel to blot. Be sure all edges are glued securely.

Procedure:
For Intermediate and Advanced, point out the two steps of the exercise: (1.) finding the matching pairs and (2.) placing them together so that patterns they share are completed. For Beginners, pairing of the sticks is enough. They may stack pairs together, and 8 pairs are probably enough.

Shape Sticks

Level:
> Intermediate-Advanced

Objective:
> To match pairs of sticks containing like shape combinations.

Skills:
> Attention to detail, visual perception

Vocabulary:
> Heart, arrow, triangle, etc.—all shape names

Materials:
> • 24 tongue depressors
>
> • Permanent colored markers
>
> • Storage container

Construction:
> Make two sticks of each combination below, using two colors for each stick.
>
> Design combinations:
>
> half moon—triangle   triangle—semi-circle   arrow—rectangle
> star—diamond   square—half-moon   cross—square
> heart—star   rectangle—cross   semi-circle—circle
> circle—oval   diamond—arrow   oval—heart

Procedure:
> Place sticks on the worksurface in random order and match pairs by stacking them together. Point out the need to observe both designs, not just one, in making matches.

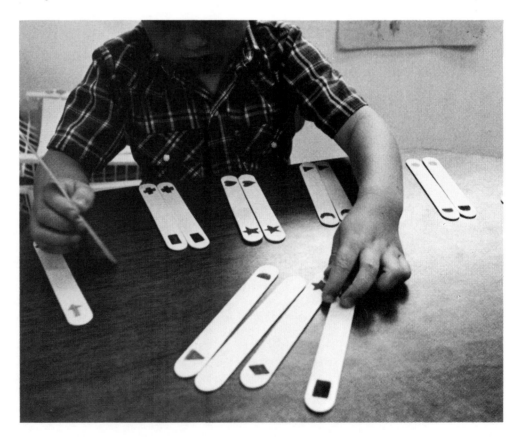

Feeling Sticks

Level:
Intermediate-Advanced

Objective:
To match pairs of sticks tactually with the eyes closed.

Skills:
Tactile discrimination, concentration

Vocabulary:
Smooth, sort, rough, ''bumpy'', etc.

Materials:
- 6 kinds of textured fabrics—felt, vinyl, burlap, satin, corduroy, velvet, etc.
- 12 tongue depressors
- White glue
- Storage container

Construction:
Cut two strips of each fabric, 5/8'' (16mm) wide and 5'' (127mm) long, using pinking shears if possible. Brush white glue generously on the sticks, all the way to both side edges and to within ¼'' (6mm) of the ends. Center the fabric strips and press firmly. Blot by pressing on a paper towel. Be sure all edges are glued securely.

Procedure:
A friend's assistance is needed to do this exercise, so ask another person to help you with the demonstration. Divide the sticks into two identical sets. The helper places one stick from each set in each of your hands. Rub them carefully with your fingers, with eyes closed. If they feel the same open your eyes and set the match aside. If ''No,'' keep eyes closed, hand one back, and keep one. Your friend gives you a second one from the same set. Continue until all

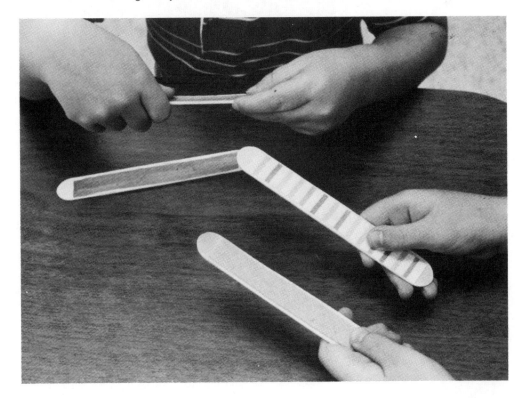

are paired. Repeat as many times as desired. Exchange roles if your friend wants to work the exercise. The person who took the exercise from the shelf puts it away.

Note: FEELING STICKS can also be made with sewing trims—lace, rick-rack, braid, ribbon, etc. Make and use them the same way.

Rods

Level:
Intermediate-Advanced

Objective:
To find the RODS which are identical in diameter and connect them, using the Velcro fasteners on the ends.

Skills:
Size discrimination, observation of graduation, comparing, ordering

Vocabulary:
Rough, smooth

Materials:
- The other half of the dowels used for CYLINDERS
- 8'' (20cm) strip of Velcro fastener, ¾'' (19mm) or 1'' (25mm) wide
- Contact cement or epoxy glue
- Storage container

Construction:

Cut the half dowels into thirds. With scissors, cut the Velcro in half lengthwise, cutting both pieces at one time. Cut the strips into pieces, 5/8'' (16mm)-¾'' (19mm) wide for the larger dowels and 3/8'' (10mm) - ½'' (13mm) for the smaller ones. There should be 12 pieces. Put contact cement or epoxy generously on the ends of the RODS and the backs of the separated Velcro pieces. Follow contact cement package directions for adhering. Attach the Velcro like this: on one of each size, (6 in all) put a ''rough'' piece of Velco on one end and a ''smooth'' piece on the other. On six of the remaining pieces, put a ''rough'' piece on one end, nothing on the other. On the last 6, put a ''smooth'' piece on one end, nothing on the other. Dry thoroughly, then trim the Velcro to fit where necessary.

Procedure:

Find matching pieces and connect them. Order them on the worksurface from small to large and reversed if desired. Using RODS on a mat rather than a table will prevent them from rolling.

Sorting

Sorting is such an absorbing activity, you may want to devote an entire shelf to it. You can have a wide variety of sorting objects and change them often, adding new ones as you find them. Some children will watch the shelf and delight in new objects to sort. The list of possible sorting objects is endless: two or more of any like discarded items are all that's needed. They're sorted by color, size, or any other feature they have in common. Here's a list to get you started: pasta (all shapes), buttons, poker chips, hardware items, office supplies, colored plastic clothespins, felt cutouts, dried beans, nuts, dollhouse miniatures, wooden mill ends, bottle caps, playing cards, dominoes, and on and on.

SORTERS will add a great deal to this activity. While it's true that SORTING need be no more complicated than grouping like objects together, a SORTER adds definition. Provide a muffin tin, felt squares, wood, plastic or metal macrame rings and small bowls and let children choose the SORTER they want to use.

Notes:

Dexterity

Children's play is also their work. We sometimes assume that if they enjoy what they're doing, they can't be learning! Nothing could be further from the truth. What supremely good luck it is that children educate themselves if they are allowed to do so. "DO TOUCH!" signs should surround them wherever they go!

DEXTERITY exercises are so much fun, adults may think of them as play. That's all right. Some of them are all process; they have no point of completion. That's all right, too. As long as activities contain two vital elements—possibility and limitations—we needn't worry; they're legitimate vehicles for learning. Skill development goals are obvious in some DEXTERITY exercises, but these exercises deserve no greater respect as serious learning tools than the "fun" ones. They are all ways of learning through the hands.

Pegboard

Level:
  Beginning to Advanced

Objective:
  To use golf tees as pegs in pegboard activities.

Skills:
  Fitting, designing patterns, color sorting

Vocabulary:
  Tees, pegs, pegboard, rows

Materials:
  - ¼'' (6mm) thick pegboard, 12'' (30.5cm) square
  - 144 golf tees, 1 7/8'' (4.8mm) long
  - White glue, contact cement or epoxy glue
  - Tinker Toys, optional
  - 18'' (45.7cm) length of 1'' × 2'' (2.5cm × 5cm) board
  - Sandpaper
  - Storage container

Construction:
  For safety's sake, blunt the points of the tees by rubbing them a few times over sandpaper, holding them straight up and down. Cut the 1'' × 2'' (2.5cm × 5cm) in half crosswise, making two 9'' (22.9cm) runners. Glue them on the underside of the pegboard, centering them between rows of holes.

  Note: Make several PEGBOARDS if you like, and draw outlines on them with a marker, to be filled in or followed with tees. To avoid having to make runners for

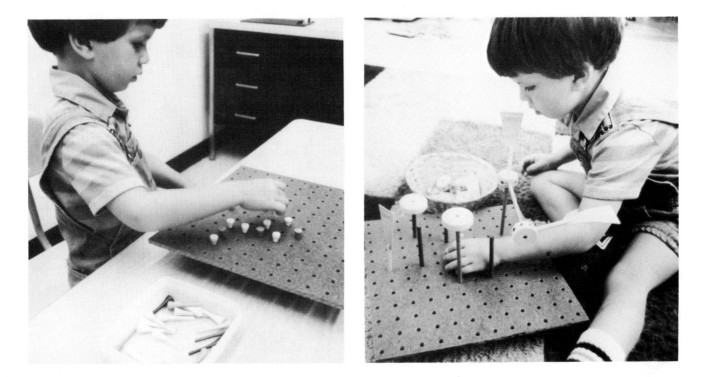

each one, glue 4 runners together to make a square base and set a board on it for use. Or use the boards with ½'' (12.7mm) diameter beads and no runners will be needed. Don't use beads with Beginners or children of any age who are likely to put them in their mouths.

Procedure:
Children seem to be born knowing how to use pegs and pegboards. Any way is fine—random placement, sorting by color, sorting into rows, making designs. Tinker Toys fit the holes in ¼'' (6mm) thick pegboard, so interesting vertical sculptures can be built on the pegboard base.

Geoboard

Level:
Beginning to Advanced

Objective:
To stretch rubber bands across the nails in various patterns.

Skills:
Making and observing linear shapes, designing and altering patterns

Vocabulary:
Rubber bands, stretch, opposite

Materials:
- A piece of board 10'' (25cm) square and 1'' (2.5cm) thick
- 81 finishing nails, 1'' (2.5cm) long
- Rubber bands
- Storage container

Construction:
Use a pencil and ruler to make marks one inch (2.5cm) apart horizontally and vertically on the entire top surface of the board, 9 in each direction. Put a nail at each mark.

Procedure:
Keep the demonstration brief for this activity. Leave room for discovery. Show how to stretch the rubber bands around two or more nails and how to overlap them. Remove the bands for storage.

Pipe

Level:
Beginning to Advanced

Objective:
To build free-standing structures with PVC pipe.

Skills:
Spatial relationship, fitting, logic, reason

Vocabulary:
Pipe, tees, crosses, ells, caps

Materials:
- 2 lengths of unthreaded PVC coldwater pipe, 6' (1.80m) long and ¾'' (19mm) in diameter

- Fittings—3 each, tees, crosses, ells, and caps—¾'' (19mm) in diameter

- Storage container

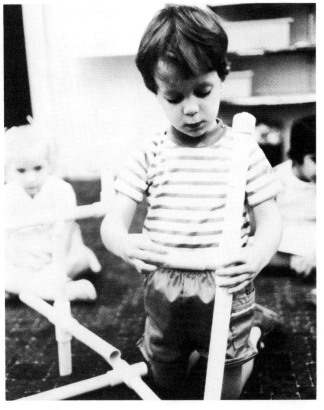

Construction:
Use a hacksaw or an electric saw to cut each pipe into 9 pieces, three of each length: 4'' (10cm), 8'' (20cm), and 12'' (30cm). Inquire about having the pipe cut where you buy it; some places will do this for you.

Procedure:
Here's an activity you can expand to your heart's content. Pipe is a wonderful basic building material, similar to hardwood unit blocks, but much less expensive. Its inventive possibilities are almost endless. Make it a group activity, if you like, by doubling or tripling the materials called for above. The set shown is an individual activity. Children can drop a marble through a finished structure, tilt it in different directions, and make it emerge at one of the open ends. Remind children that pipe structures are not strong enough for climbing.

Hardware Board

Level:
Intermediate-Advanced

Objective:
To use hand tools to attach hardware to the pegboard.

Skills:
Familiarity with hardware and tools, manual dexterity

Vocabulary:
Screwdriver, pliers, nuts, bolts, wing nut, etc.

Materials:
- ¼'' (6mm) thick pegboard, 6'' × 12'' (15cm × 30cm)
- Assorted hardware—nuts, bolts, wing nuts, knobs, etc.—all ¼'' (6mm) diameter
- Short-handled screwdriver
- Small pliers
- Storage container

Construction:
None required.

Procedure:
It's tricky to learn how to put a nut and bolt together without crossing the threads, but most children like to try. If, during the demonstration, you point out the need to stop and begin again when the nut doesn't turn easily, frustration can be avoided. Attach the hardware to the board in any way that pleases. It should be removed for storage.

Modeling Dough

Do all teachers have a recurring nightmare in which their class is suddenly in a state of total, terrifying anarchy? I do—but once, in the dream, I magically produced a supply of modeling dough and saved the day! They fell on the bright blue mass so eagerly, peace was restored in an instant! That's not far removed from reality, either; modeling dough does seem to have near-magic appeal, and its versatility continually surprises me. I've even used it at birthday parties for my own children when they were very young. After a play session at the kitchen table, I gave the guests containers of it, freshly-made from the recipe I give here, with copies of the recipe for their mothers. Incidentally, this is the very best recipe I've ever found, and I've tried several. The uncooked kinds are faster to make, but not nearly so pliable and long-lasting. This one cooks over high heat in a flash, so it really is worth the bit of extra effort. Here it is:

Modeling Dough

1 cup flour
½ cup salt
2 teaspoons cream of tartar
1 cup water
1 tablespoon cooking oil
Food coloring

Mix dry ingredients, add liquids and cook over high heat til it forms a ball, stirring constantly. Lumps will disappear. Recipe may be doubled. Needs no refrigeration; store covered.

The way I recommend using modeling dough in the classroom is different from the usual way. It's not a group activity, but an individualized one. As such, it requires dough in continuous supply, but since it lasts so well it need be made up only once a month or so. Double the recipe and store the unused portion for future use. Be generous with the amount for the exercise. This full recipe is just right. Keep it in a covered container on the modeling dough tray—it doesn't need refrigeration and it will stay soft indefinitely. If more than one color is used at a time, the colors will be mixed during use and produce an unappetizing muddy hue. Better to rotate colors, and the brighter they are, the longer they will stay fresh-looking.

Caution students in the pre-use demonstration to stay seated while they're using modeling dough, and enforce this rule, or bits of it will begin turning up everywhere.

Purists will say nothing should be added to modeling dough but children's hands, but most of us can't resist adding some accessories. Since it's not an art activity, but an exercise in dexterity, I feel accessories enhance its value. If you agree, rotate the MODELING DOUGH TOOLS (directions follow) and these combinations of kitchen utensils:

1. cookie cutters, a wide spatula and the roller (see MODELING DOUGH TOOLS)
2. a pastry cutting wheel and the roller
3. a meatballer or melon baller
4. a tube-type cake decorator
5. a garlic press and table knife

Store the accessories you are currently using with the modeling dough, in a covered container, on a tray on the workshelf.

Modeling Dough Tools

Level:
Beginning to Advanced

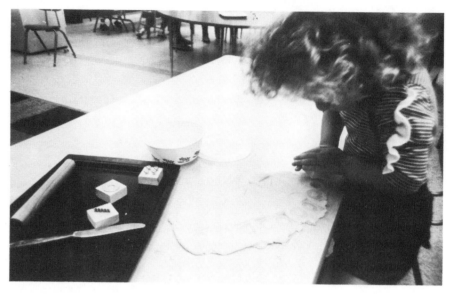

Objective:
To use the roller and stamps with MODELING DOUGH.

Skills:
Observing cause-effect, observing alterations in shape and form, initiating design, manual dexterity

Vocabulary:
Stamp, roller, roll, design

Materials:
- A piece of 1'' × 2'' (2.5cm × 5cm) board, 6'' (15cm) long
- Large washer
- Large nut (hardware)
- 4 short nails
- Corrugated nail or other hardware
- Epoxy or other metal bonding glue
- An 8''–12'' (20cm-30cm) long piece of wooden dowel 1'' (2.5cm) in diameter or larger
- Covered storage container
- Tray

Construction:
Cut the length of 1'' × 2'' (2.5cm × 5cm) into 4 pieces, each 1½'' (38mm) long. Glue a washer on one and a nut on another. Hammer the 4 nails into one, allowing them to extend ¼'' (6mm). Hammer the corrugated nail into the last stamp allowing it to extend ¼'' (6mm).

Procedure:
Children can use the roller (an adult rolling pin may be substituted) to flatten the MODELING DOUGH to use with the stamps. A table knife is a good accompaniment. Store the tools with the MODELING DOUGH, in a covered container, on the tray.

Sand

Beginning to Advanced:

Sand is not just for outdoors! It's also a wonderful indoor DEXTERITY exercise. Don't be afraid of messiness! It is not *very* messy, and children clean their own space after using it. All you need are a container such as a cat litter tray, sand, and accessories which you can easily collect. The sand should be fine-grained and free of debris. Sift if necessary. Bags of play sand can be bought at home centers or hardware stores. Children may need help carrying it. Remind them that only the sand equipment may be used in the sand, nothing else.

Provide two types of sand accessories—for WET (DAMP) SAND and for DRY SAND. They have distinctly different properties: when sand is damp, it can be molded and will hold a shape. Dry, it's a flowing medium with a different set of possibilities.

WET SAND—You need some kind of sprinkler to dampen the sand. A push-in sprinkler top (used for dampening clothes before ironing) in a bottle of water works well. Children should ask an adult to sprinkle the sand when they wish to use it damp.

Anything that will make a shape can be used with wet sand: gelatin molds, muffin tins, plastic ice cube trays, heavyweight plastic glasses or cups and so on. Collect as many as possible and rotate 3 or 4 at at time.

DRY SAND—Rotate SAND COMBS (see next exercise) with dipping and pouring utensils, such as spoons and plastic bowls or cups, and a shaker made from a plastic cup with holes punched in the bottom.

Sand Combs

Level:
Beginning to Advanced

Objective:
To make configurations in sand with the combs.

Skills:
Experiencing form and pattern, control of a creative medium

Vocabulary:
Pull, push, lightly, curve, swirl

Materials:
• 3 large (approximately 6'' [16.2cm] in diameter) plastic snap-on lids from food containers

Construction:
Use scissors to cut the plastic lids in half, making one in a wave pattern, one a zig-zag, and one a square-wave (corrugated) pattern.

Procedure:
Make curving, swirling motions with the combs in sand. (See the SAND exercise.) Try straight and angled motions, too. Shake the pan gently to redistribute and level the sand.

Insets and Templates

Objective:
To trace around the templates and inside the insets using colored pencils.

Skills:
Eye-hand coordination, small muscle discipline, reward through attention to detail

Vocabulary:
Trace, inside, outside

Materials:
- 6 to 12 medium to large plastic snap-on lids from food containers—all the same size
- Paper squares
- Colored pencils
- Single-edge razor blade
- 3 containers: one each for insets and templates; one for pencils

Construction:
Use any or all of these shapes or your own: cross, heart, clover, triangle, semicircle, V, rectangle, circle, diamond, oval, half-moon, star. Symmetrical shapes are easier to cut from paper than to draw; start with squares of paper the same size and fold in half to cut. Trace around the shapes on the lids with ball point pen and cut with the razor blade. Cut the edges off the lids or leave them. Store appropriate-sized paper with the exercise.

Procedure:
It's possible to make insets and templates at the same time, using 6 lids. You may cut both at the same time; the cut-outs become TEMPLATES. But for variety, you may want to use different shapes for each set, if you do, make 6 for insets, 6 for templates, using all the suggested shapes. Children trace around

templates, inside insets—each requires different handling and motions. Both foster fine motor coordination and control, which are good preparation for writing. I like to introduce tracing in two phases. During the first phase, children learn the tracing technique and gain control. For this, single tracings are best, on small squares of paper which will hold one tracing. In the second phase, three insets or templates may be used, on larger pieces of paper, to make superimposed tracings or one may be used in three overlapped positions. In both phases, the technique is the same—trace slowly and carefully, connecting the beginning of the line with the end. Then the tracing may be colored with the pencils. Greater proficiency with a pencil can be achieved by making deliberate, back-and-forth motions, with the strokes going in one direction. This is not the same way children use crayons, which is in several directions. I'm not in favor of rigidly enforcing the suggested method; good experience is gained either way; but children will usually follow the example you give in the demonstration.

Use INSETS and TEMPLATES as separate exercises, and rotate three of each at a time.

Chains

Level:
Intermediate-Advanced

Objective:
To form interlocking links with the belt backing and fasteners.

Skills:
Enjoyment of altering shape and function, fitting, progression

Vocabulary:
Chain, link, fastener

Materials:
- 2 yds. (1.8m) white plastic belting ¾'' (19mm) wide from a fabric store
- 2 yds. (1.8m)d black plastic belting ¾'' (19mm) wide from a fabric store
- Brass paper fasteners
- Paper hole punch
- 2 storage containers, one small, one large

Construction:
Cut the belting into 10'' (25cm) lengths. Use the hole punch to make holes ¾'' (19mm) from both ends of each piece.

Procedure:
Producing a chain with these links is not the purpose of this activity; linking them together and experiencing progression is. Alternate colors or not as you make the chain. Take all loops apart before returning the materials to the shelf. Put fasteners in the small container, put it and the strips in the larger one.

Weaving Board

Level:
Intermediate-Advanced

Objective:
To weave the ribbons over and under the fixed elastic bands.

Skills:
Manual dexterity, color selection, satisfaction of creation

Vocabulary:
Weave, ribbons, elastic

Materials:
- A piece of board, 10'' (25cm) square, and 1'' (2.5cm) thick
- 3 yards (2.7m) of 1'' (2.5cm) wide elastic
- Heavy duty staple gun or hammer-in staples
- Grosgrain ribbon in varied widths, assorted colors, 12'' (30.5cm) lengths
- White glue
- Storage container

Construction:
Cut the elastic into 12'' (30.5cm) lengths. Place them on the board, side by side, stretching slightly to overlap each end one inch (2.5cm) on the back of the board. Double-staple each end, firmly to the back of the board. Trim the cut ends of the ribbons evenly and dip the last ¼'' (6mm) of each end into white glue to prevent fraying.

Procedure:
Show the basic over-and-under technique for weaving. Point out the alternating pattern which is created, and that each new row begins the opposite way from the last. Stress the importance of removing the ribbons before returning the loom to the shelf. Students may want to try weaving with scrap yarn or paper strips after learning the technique.

Snapping Bar

Level:
Beginning to Advanced

Objective:
To snap the two strips of snap tape together.

Skills:
Precision, coordination, perception

Vocabulary:
Snaps

Materials:
- A piece of 1'' × 2'' (2.5cm × 5cm) board, 18'' (46cm) long
- 18'' (26cm) of snap tape, from a fabric store, see note below
- Heavy duty staple gun or hammer-in staples

Construction:
Separate the snap tape strips and center one of them on the board lengthwise. Staple both sides and ends to the board, close to the edge, making the staples no more than an inch apart. Snap the other strip on and double staple one end to the board, through both thicknesses. (On the other end, only the bottom strip is stapled, to allow the strips to be separated.)

Procedure:
The exercise should be put away with the two strips snapped together, if possible. To begin, unsnap them, and beginning at the top, match the two parts of each snap. Point out the need to snap each pair in succession. Repeat as desired.

Note: Several kinds of snap tape are available. The larger the snap, the easier it will be, so keep this in mind when making your selection. Beginners will need the largest snaps—advanced the smallest.

Braiding Bar

Level:
Intermediate-Advanced

Objective:
To learn the art of braiding.

Skills:
Braiding technique, manual dexterity

Vocabulary:
Braiding, cords, elastic band

Materials:
- A piece of 1'' × 2'' (2.5cm × 5cm) board, 18'' (46cm) long
- 3 lengths of braided satin cord, (or other heavy cord) each 18'' (46cm) long, each piece a different color
- 4'' (10cm) elastic, any width
- Heavy duty staple gun or hammer-in staples
- Clear plastic tape or cellophane tape, optional

Construction:
Wrap the ends of the cord with tape, tightly, several times, to prevent fraying, or machine stitch a half-inch (13mm) from the ends. Staple one end of each cord at one end of the board, placing the cords side by side. Attach the elastic band at the other end of the board, stretching it around to the back and stapling it on the back side.

Procedure:
Slowly show the way to braid: separate the cords so one is in the middle and one on each side. Lift each of the outside cords in turn and place over the center one. Continue until braided to the end. Separate the strands and tuck the ends under the elastic band before putting the bar away.

Lace Boards

Level:
 Beginning to Advanced

Objective:
 To lace the pegboard squares together in a variety of ways.

Skills:
 Small muscle control, precision, symmetry

Vocabulary:
 Lace, box

Materials:
- 6 pieces of 1/4'' (6mm) or 1/8'' (3mm) thick pegboard, 4'' × 4'' (10cm × 10cm) 6 (3 pairs) 18'' (45.7cm) long shoelaces
- Storage container

Construction:
 Cut the squares from pegboard, sawing between rows of holes.

Procedure:
 Show the different ways the squares can be connected:
 1. laced together in a line;
    connect the ends to make a circle
 2. laced together to make a box
 3. laced together in random
    arrangement
 A 2'' (5.1cm) length of the lace should be left at the beginning, to prevent its pulling out. There are several ways to lace: running stitch (in-and-out), overcast (diagonal), and across (makes a straight line). Stress the need to avoid skipping holes. Remove laces before storing the exercise.

 Note for Beginners: Young Beginners probably won't be able to connect these squares, but can enjoy lacing, so a larger board, perhaps 12'' × 12'' (30.5cm × 30.5cm) or so, which they can lace in-and-out, is appropriate for them. Draw free-form designs on it with a marker if you like, to be followed with the lace.

Lacing Bar

Level:

Beginning to Advanced

Objective:

To lace the shoelace through the eyelets, in an alternating pattern.

Skills:

Lacing, alternating, eye-hand coordination

Vocabulary:

Lace, eyelets

Materials:

- A piece of 1''×2'' (2.5cm×5cm) board, 18'' (46cm) long

- 1 hammer-in staple or heavy duty staple gun

- 54'' (137cm) long athletic shoelace or two shoelaces 27'' (68.5cm) long

- 16 small screw eyes

Construction:

Put two rows of screw eyes every 2'' (5cm) on the board, ¼'' (6mm) from each edge. If a 54'' (137cm) lace is used, center it at the top of the board and staple it. If two 27'' (68.5cm) laces are used, overlap them and staple, cutting off the coated ends before stapling in place.

Procedure:

Have the children examine their shoes and observe how they are laced: the crossed laces form an X. Take both ends of the lace on the bar and put them through the eyelets alternately, forming X-patterns. At the end of the bar, children who know how may tie a bow. Those who don't know how may use the bar to learn, with an adult's assistance; or they may leave the ends untied. Unlace the bar before returning it to the shelf.

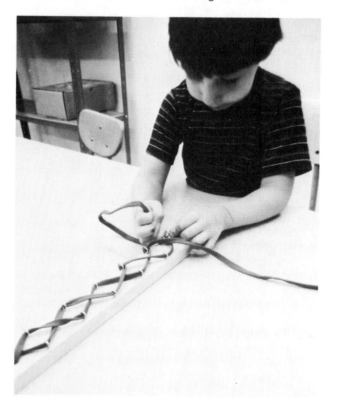

Chip Bowl and Bean Bowl

Level:
Beginning-Intermediate
(see note below)

Objective:
To drop poker chips, one at a time, through a slot in the bowl lid; to drop dried beans, one at a time, through a hole in the bowl lid.

Skills:
Eye-hand coordination, fine motor control, progression, completion

Vocabulary:
Chip, bowl, slot, bean, names of colors if used

Materials:
- A plastic bowl with a snap-on lid for each exercise
- Single-edge razor blade
- Poker chips
- Large dried lima beans

Construction:
With the razor blade, cut a slot which is slightly larger than a poker chip in the center of one of the bowl lids. Cut a 1'' (2.54cm) diameter hole in the center of the other bowl lid.

Procedure:
These are basic repetitive activities for the youngest, although CHIP BOWL may be adapted for older children. Use them as separate activities. (See note below.) To use either exercise: remove the chips or beans from the bowl (where they

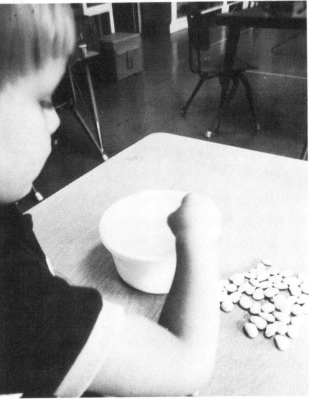

are stored) and snap the lid back on. Drop the chips through the slot, or the beans through the hole one at a time and repeat as desired.

Have enough chips or beans to maintain interest, but not so many that some are left unused. Consider the ages of the children. CHIP BOWL can be adapted for Beginners to include sorting, by making it as for Intermediates—see note below.

Note for Intermediates: Adapt CHIP BOWL by providing a bowl for each color chip used. Use permanent markers to make a band of color around the outside of each bowl to match the colors of the chips.

Safety note: Use only large beans for BEAN BOWL; do not use the activity with children who are likely to put the beans in their mouths.

Tee Bowl

Level:
Beginning-Intermediate

Objective:
To fit the golf tees into the holes in the bowl lid.

Skills:
Fitting, arranging, manual dexterity

Vocabulary:
Tees

Materials:
- Large plastic bowl with a snap-on lid
- Golf tees
- Paper hole punch
- Sandpaper

Construction:
Blunt the points of the tees by rubbing them back and forth a few times over sandpaper, holding them straight up and down. Use the hole punch to make holes around the edge of the lid, just inside the rim, spacing them an inch (2.5cm) apart. You will have to wedge the rim of the lid into the hole punch for the first hole, then slide it to the next position, and the next, without removing it.

Procedure:
The golf tees can be stored in the bowl. For use, remove them, snap the lid back on, and put the tees one at a time in the holes in the top. Several bowls may be used if you wish to sort by color; provide the correct number of each color of golf tees to fill the holes in each bowl. Designate the bowls by color by making a band of color around the outside of the bowl with permanent colored markers.

Hammerboard

Level:
Beginning to Advanced
(See note for
Beginners below)

Objective:
To hammer golf tees into the pegboard in three different activities.

Skills:
Spatial involvement, arrangement

Vocabulary:
Geoboard, elastic, stretch, loops, arches, tees

Materials:
- 1/8'' (3mm) thick pegboard, 16'' × 24'' (40.6cm × 61cm)
- A piece of 1'' × 2'' (2.5cm × 5cm) board, 36'' (91.4cm) long
- 1/8'' (3mm) wide elastic: 2 yds. (183cm) black, 2 yds. (183cm) white
- Golf tees, 1 7/8'' (4.8cm) long
- 1/2'' (12.7mm) or 3/4'' (19mm) wide white plastic belting, 3 yds. (2.7m)—fabric store
- Paper hole punch
- Food coloring
- White glue, contact cement or epoxy glue
- Small hammer or toy hammer
- Containers

Construction:
Saw the 1'' × 2'' (2.5cm × 5cm) into 3 runners, each 12'' (30.5cm) long, and glue them to the underside of the pegboard, between rows of holes—one near each end and one in the middle. Cut the belting into strips, 8'', 12'' and 18'' (20.3,

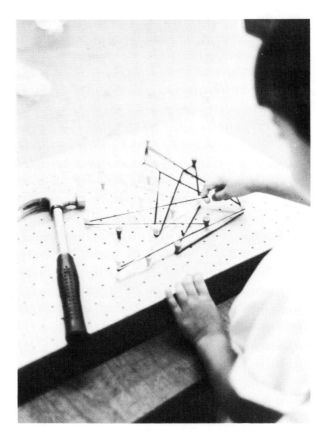

30.5, and 45.7 cm) long and use the hole punch to make a hole ½'' (12.7mm) from each end. Put an additional hole in the center of the long strips. Dye the strips pastel hues by dipping them in food-color/water solutions. Knot the ends of the elastic tightly to form two bands. Blunt the tips of the golf tees by rubbing them over sandpaper a few times, holding them straight up and down.

Procedure:
Notice that the HAMMERBOARD is made of 1/8'' (3mm) thick pegboard, while the 12'' × 12'' (30.5cm × 30.5cm) PEGBOARD is 1/4'' (6mm) thick. The thicker board has larger holes than the thinner one. Each is used to accommodate the golf tees in a different way; they must fit loosely in the small PEGBOARD and tightly in the HAMMERBOARD. In this activity, the tees are hammered in the board in three separate activities; to remove them, hold the board upside down and hammer them out. Don't permit rough treatment with the hammer; moderate taps are sufficient. Each activity is done separately.

1. PEGS—hammer tees in any desired order—randomly or sorted by colors, in rows, designs, etc.
2. GEOBOARD SCULPTURE—hammer tees around the board randomly. Stretch one of the elastic bands between as many tees as possible, until there is no stretch left. Repeat with the other band, arranging to your own satisfaction.
3. ARCHES—attach the belting strips to the board with the pegs, looping over and under each other, twisting for effect, etc. Try them stretched flat, too.

Note for Beginners: A smaller, 12'' × 12'' (30.5cm × 30.5cm) board made as for PEGBOARD (but using 1/8'' (3mm) thick pegboard) is a good HAMMERBOARD for Beginners. Use it only for the PEGS activity if the other two activities are too advanced.

Ramp

Level:
Beginning

Objective:
To roll the balls down the ramp.

Skills:
Balance, manual dexterity, control

Vocabulary:
Ramp, sponge

Materials:
- 18'' (45.7cm) length of narrow (approximately 1'' (2.54cm) wide) wood cove molding (or other molding)
- 2 or more small balls
- 2 polyfoam (not cellulose) sponges
- Storage container

Construction:
Use scissors to cut the sponges in half crosswise. Cut a piece out of one of the long sides of one, approximately an inch (2.5cm) deep and the width of the molding. To use, stack the sponges so that they support the molding at one end, forming a ramp for the balls.

Repetition is not boring to very young children—they like to roll these balls down the ramp, retrieve them and roll them again and again. Demonstrate the need to stack the sponges with care so they won't topple when the ramp is positioned. The sponge with the cutout should be in the top position. Children may ask a friend to share the activity, if they like; one can be "roller" and one "catcher." Store the balls separately, if necessary, for their safekeeping.

Dominoes

It surely must have been a child who invented "domino toppling"—making a standing row fall in succession by tapping the first one. It's a challenge of patience as well as coordination. Perhaps you can collect some broken sets. Combine them for toppling, making long "roads" across the floor, stacking—whatever.

Notes:

ABC's and 123's

ABC'S materials are not designed to teach reading; they're groundwork for it. A child who concludes through either casual or planned exposure to the alphabet that it's a useful thing to know, since letters make words and words make stories, has taken the first step toward reading. These exercises are means of perceiving letters through the hands, as well as through the eyes.

Children use mathematics long before they enter first grade. What child has never divided cookies among her friends or eaten half an apple? Transactions such as these are the basis for all arithmetic. Vital to this learning progression is that it moves from the concrete to the abstract, which is the natural order. 123'S materials are concrete manipulatives. Physical manipulation—increasing, decreasing, sequencing, changing quantity and volume—is the very best way to experience numbers as representations of quantity. Holding six of something in your hand makes that number your own.

Magnetic Letters

Level:
Intermediate-Advanced

Objective:
To order the magnetic alphabet on a metal sheet.

Skills:
Letter recognition, ordering

Vocabulary:
Letters of the alphabet

Materials:
- 26'' (66cm) of magnetic tape—hobby or handicraft stores
- ¾'' (19mm) wide white or colored plastic tape
- Permanent colored markers
- Storage container

Construction:
Peel off the paper on the top side of the magnetic tape and replace it with the plastic tape; trim the excess. Cut into 1'' (2.5cm) pieces and print the upper case (and lower case, if used) on them with the colored markers.

Procedure:
This exercise uses the cookie sheet (non-aluminum) which is used with several other exercises. Separate and spread the letters face-up on the worksurface. Order from a to z by attaching them in horizontal or vertical rows on the metal cookie sheet. A variation for matching upper and lower case letters can be made—use a different color tape for lower case. You will need twice as much magnetic tape. A poster of the alphabet should be visible in the room.

Magnetic Numbers

Level:
Intermediate-Advanced

Objective:
To order the magnetic numbers from one to a hundred on the metal sheet.

Skills:
Counting, observation of decades, organizing

Vocabulary:
Conversation pertinent to performing the exercise

Materials:

- 1 roll (60''(152.4cm) of ½'' (12.7mm) wide magnetic tape
- 1 roll colored plastic tape, ¾'' (19mm) wide
- Permanent colored markers
- Storage container

Construction:
Adhere the magnetic tape to the cookie sheet for easy handling. Peel the paper backing from it and replace it with the colored plastic tape, allowing it to extend over one edge. Trim the excess. With scissors, cut the magnetic tape into ½'' (12.7mm) squares. Use a different colored marker to write the numbers of each decade;—e.g. red for 1–10, blue for 11–20, etc. Or, to raise the level of difficulty, make them all one color.

Procedure:
Use the cookie sheet (non-aluminum) which is used with several different exercises. Remove the numbers from the storage container and spread them face

up, in random order, on the worksurface. The numbers of each decade are of the same color to simplify grouping. Point out the need for orderly arrangement and spacing. The numbers from one to ten are on the first row; those from eleven to twenty on the second and so on—ten rows of ten. For inexperienced counters, also point out that the ones are aligned vertically, the twos, and so on. The level of difficulty can be raised by making all the numbers in the same color. Remove the numbers from the sheet before putting the materials away.

Counting Rods

Level:
Intermediate-Advanced

Objective:
To place the right number of counters on each rod, from 1 to 10.

Skills:
Progression, counting, adding

Vocabulary:
Counters, rods

Materials:
- 2 wooden dowels, each 5/16'' (7.9mm) diameter
- A 30'' (76.2cm) piece of vinyl tubing, ½'' (12.7mm) inside diameter, preferably opaque—hardware store or home center
- Storage container

Construction:
Saw ten 7'' (17.8cm) long rods from the dowels. Use scissors to cut 55 pieces, each ½'' (12.7mm) wide from the tubing.

Procedure:
Thread one counter on a rod and place it on the worksurface. Thread two on the next, and place it underneath or beside the first one. Continue to ten.

Abacus

Level:
Intermediate-Advanced

Objective:
To thread the rubber hose washers on the rod, putting the correct number in the spaces.

Skills:
Counting, number sequence, grouping

Vocabulary:
Washers

Materials:
- 55 rubber hose washers
- 5/8'' (16mm) diameter wooden dowel, 22'' (55cm) long
- Permanent colored markers
- Container for washers

Construction:
Use a pencil and ruler to mark the rod as follows: leave an inch (2.5cm) on each end and between each space for the washers. Make the first mark an inch (2.5cm) from one end of the rod, the second mark ¼ inch (6mm) from that. This is the space for the first washer. Skip another inch (2.5cm), then mark the second space 3/8'' (9.5mm) wide. This is the space for two washers. Continue to ten, leaving these spaces for the washers: Number 3—½'' (1.27cm); number 4—¾'' (19mm); number 5—1'' (2.5cm); number 6—1 ¼'' (3.1cm); number 7—1 3/8'' (3.49cm); number 8—1 ½'' (3.8cm); number 9—1 ¾'' (4.45cm); number 10—2'' (5cm). Use the permanent colored markers to color in the inch (2.5cm)-wide spaces between the washer positions.

Procedure:
Hold the rod with the narrowest band at the left (for a right-handed person), then slip one washer on the opposite end and slide it to the narrowest band, which is the number one position. Repeat with two washers, three and so on to ten. Try the exercise counting backwards from ten, too, by reversing the orientation of the rod and placing ten washers first, then nine, etc.

Rulers

Level:
Intermediate-Advanced

Objective:
To "measure" things in the room—tables, the width of the room, people, etc.

Skills:
Distance awareness, relating numbers to distance, spatial awareness

Vocabulary:
Feet, inches, ruler

Materials:
- 6 wooden yardsticks
- Storage container

Construction:
Cut the yardsticks into thirds at the 12" and 24" marks.

Procedure:
Lay the rulers end to end to "measure." No need to total up the inches and feet—the idea is to sense measurement and distance—did this table use more rulers that that one? "The room is so big, we had to pick up all the rulers and put them down again,"—these kinds of comparisons.

Rhyming

Level:
Intermediate-Advanced

Objective:
To pair pictures and objects which rhyme.

Skills:
Sound recognition, picture recognition, rhyming

Vocabulary:
Rhyme, names of all objects and pictures

Materials:
- Pictures: pan, moon, pail, cap, coat, mop, ring, sock, clock, rug, ten (the number), lamp, star, tree—choose any 10—try children's workbooks
- Objects: can (small juice), spoon, nail, map (small piece), toy boat, toy top, rock, toy bug, pen, stamp, toy car, key, map, string—choose 10 to rhyme with pictures
- Clear plastic
- Clear plastic adhesive
- 2 storage containers

Construction:
Put the stamp on a small card and laminate it and all the pictures as described under LAMINATING in PUTTING IT ALL TOGETHER

Procedure:
Separate the pictures and objects on the worksurface. Put the objects (or pictures) in a row. Match the pictures (or objects) according to their rhyming sounds. Much preparation is necessary for this exercise. Spend adequate time in the demonstration discussing rhyming sounds. Be sure students are thoroughly familiar with all pictures and objects and their names.

Store the objects in a small container; put it inside a larger container which also holds the pictures.

Sticks and Circles

Level:
Advanced

Objective:
To make the lower case alphabet using circles (and their fractions) and straight pieces.

Skills:
Observing letter formations, ordering the alphabet

Vocabulary:
Sticks, circles, names of letters

Materials:
- Felt in three colors
- Iron-on interfacing, heavyweight, optional
- Storage container

Construction:
Apply iron-on interfacing, if it is to be used, before cutting the felt. Make whole and half-sticks in one color felt; whole and half circles of a second color; fourths and three-fourths sticks and circles of the third color. Make patterns for sticks: cut a whole one 4'' (10cm) long, ½'' (1.27cm) wide. Fold and cut to make halves, fourths, and three-fourths. Use these to cut all other sticks. Make patterns for circles: cut a whole one 2'' (5cm) outside diameter. Cut a 1'' (2.5cm) hole in the center. (Use two of these cut-outs for dots for the i and j.) Fold a circle and cut in halves, fourths and three-fourths. Use these as patterns to cut all other circles.

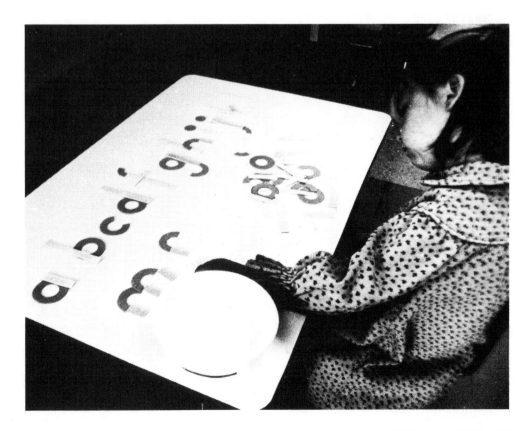

Make this number of each:

	Sticks	Circles
Whole	7	7
½	18	7
¼	10	5
¾	5	2

Procedure:

This exercise is an especially effective way to familiarize children with the formation of lower case printed letters. They're all made from the basic forms of "sticks" and "circles." However, it is meaningful only when the lower case alphabet is being actively taught. The felt will adhere slightly to a carpet mat, so that is a better worksurface than a tabletop. Make a 3-color poster, using the same colors as the felt, showing how to form the letters, and put it on a wall to be used as a guide. To assemble the cut shapes to make the alphabet, use the following:

a: 1 whole circle, ½ stick
b: 1 whole stick, 1 whole circle
c: ¾ circle
d: 1 whole stick, 1 whole circle
e: ¾ circle, ½ stick
f: ¾ stick, ¼ stick, ¼ circle
g: 1 whole circle, ¾ stick, ¼ circle
h: 1 whole stick, ½ circle, ¼ stick
i: ½ stick, dot (center of a circle)
j: ¾ stick, ¼ circle, dot
k: 1 whole stick, ¼ sticks, ½ stick
l: 1 whole stick
m: two ½ circles, three ¼ sticks

n: ½ circle, two ¼ sticks
o: 1 whole circle
p: 1 whole circle, 1 whole stick
q: 1 whole circle, ¾ stick, ¼ circle
r: ½ stick, ¼ circle
s: two ½ circles
t: ¾ stick, ½ stick
u: ½ circle, two ¼ sticks
v: two ½ sticks
w: four ½ sticks
x: two ½ sticks
y: 1 whole stick, ½ stick
z: three ½ sticks

Counting Bar

Level:
Intermediate-Advanced

Objective:
To put the correct number of closures on the nails from 1 to 10.

Skills:
Counting, ordering, increasing, left to right progression

Vocabulary:
Closures

Materials:
- 55 plastic bag closures—from supermarket produce, bread packages, etc.

- A piece of 1"×2" (2.5cm×5cm) board, 18" (45.7cm) long

- 10 cup hooks, ½" (12.7mm)

- Storage container

Construction:

Make a light pencil mark down the board lengthwise, ½'' (12.7mm) from one long edge. Make a mark 1½'' (38mm) from one end and then every 1¾'' (44.5mm) thereafter for the cup hooks. Screw in one cup hook at each mark. Use a permanent marker to write the numbers from one to ten beneath the cup hooks, holding the bar horizontally.

Procedure:

Stand the board on edge before you. Hang one closure on the nail marked one, two on the nail marked two, and so on to ten.

The exercise may be made more difficult by numbering the nails in random order, instead of in sequence. This is especially for older children.

Number Balance

Level:
Intermedidate-Advanced

Objective:
To experiment with number/position/weight relationships by changing the placement of the washers on the balance beam.

Skills:
Observing balance/imbalance, proportion, cause/effect

Vocabulary:
Washers, beam, weights, balance, level

Materials:

- An 18'' (45.7cm) length of 1'' × 2'' (2.5cm × 5cm) board
- 10 small nails
- 30 metal washers in 3 sizes, approximately 1 3/8'' (35mm), 7/8'' (22mm), 5/8'' (15.9mm)—10 of each size
- 1 screw eye
- 12'' (30.5cm) length of heavy cord
- 1 small S-hook, optional
- Storage container for the washers

Construction:

Make a pencil mark 1½'' (3.8cm) from one end of the board and every 1¾'' (4.5cm) after that, ½'' (1.3cm) from the top edge of the board, making 10 in all. Put a nail on each mark, bending each upward slightly to prevent the washers from falling off. Use a marker to write the numbers 1 to 5 under the nails, numbering from each end to the center. Put the screw eye in the center of the top edge of the board, and tie one end of the cord to the screw eye. Tie the other end to the S-hook and bend the curve closed with pliers. If no S-hook is used, tie a loop in the end of the cord.

Procedure:

Hang the BALANCE on one of the center hooks of the SUSPENSION ROD. Experiment by placing a large washer on one of the nails numbered 1. What happens to the beam? What can you do to level it? Place a large washer on one of the nails numbered 5. What happened?

Will two medium-sized washers balance a large one? How many small ones balance a medium one? Will a small one balance a medium one if it's placed in a certain position on the beam? Experiment.

Level:
Intermediate-Advanced

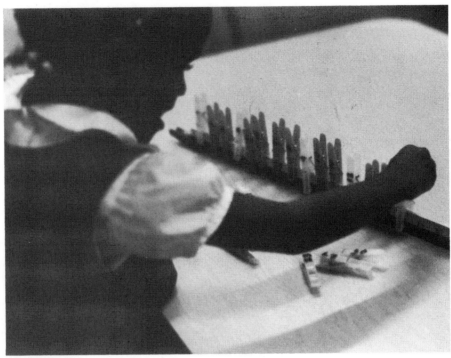

Objective:
To clip numbered clothespins on the yardstick at the corresponding numbers.

Skills:
Identifying like numbers, manual dexterity

Vocabulary:
Yardstick, clothespins, clip

Materials:
- Yardstick
- 38 colored plastic or wooden clothespins, the spring type
- Permanent colored or black markers
- Storage container

Construction:
Use colored markers for wooden clothespins, black for colored plastic clothespins. Write the numbers from 1 to 36 on the clothespins, horizontally, in order to have adequate space for double-digit numbers. Two clips will be left for the end supports.

Procedure:
Clip the two unnumbered clothespins to the ends of the yardstick, as supports. Show how clothespins are opened and closed. Let everyone try it. Clip them, one by one by one in place, matching the numbers. Children may choose to work either of two ways: by locating the #1 clip, and clipping it in place, then the #2 clip and so on; or they may clip the clothespins in random order. The yardstick may be hung on a hook on the wall if storage is a problem.

Note: The exercise can be simplified by using one color in sequence; for example, yellow clothespins for number 1–10, green for 11–20, etc.

Dot Bar

Level:

Intermediate-Advanced

Objective:

To put the tags on the board in the correct sequence, by matching the dots to numbers.

Skills:

Associating numbers and symbols, counting, left to right progression

Vocabulary:

Tags, dots

Materials:

- 10 key tags, 1¼'' (3.2cm) diameter
- Permanent colored markers
- 10 cup hooks, ½'' (12.7mm)
- A length of 1''×2'' (2.5cm×5cm) board, 18'' (45.7cm) long
- Container for key tags

Construction:

Use the markers to make dots on the tags as shown, in rows of three across, observing left to right progression. To make the board, make a pencil mark 1½'' (3.8cm) from one end of the board and every 1¾'' (4.5cm) after that, down the center of the board. Screw the cup hooks in on the marks. Use the black marker to write the numbers one through ten above each hook, keeping them small—approximately 3/8'' (9.5mm) tall.

Procedure:

Spread the tags, face up, on the worksurface. Find the tag with one dot and put it on the hook marked 1. Continue until all are placed.

First Sounds

Objective:
 To classify objects as beginning with an S-sound or a P-sound.

Skills:
 Auditory perception, sound distinction, letter-sound recognition

Vocabulary:
 Names of the objects used

Materials:
 • S objects: spoon, stick, spool, soap, stamp, sponge, salt

 • P objects: pen, pencil, penny, popcorn (popped kernels), peas (picture), paper,
      pepper (ground black)

 • Storage container

Construction:
 Laminate the popcorn, postage stamp, penny, and picture of peas according to
 directions under LAMINATING in PUTTING IT ALL TOGETHER. Use black or
 colored markers to print a large S and P on 3'' (7.6cm) square clear plastic
 squares. Put a scant ¼ teaspoon of salt under the S and ¼ teaspoon of pepper
 under the P to use as references and laminate both.

Procedure:
 Discuss S-sounds and P-sounds—a hissing sound for S, a "puh" sound for P.
 Help students to notice tongue positions for each sound. Name and discuss the
 objects in the exercise. To do the exercise place the letters on the worksurface
 side by side and place the objects one at a time in vertical rows beneath the
 appropriate letter.

1–10 Rings

Level:
Intermediate-Advanced

Objective:
To put the right number of buttons in the rings from 1 to 10 and arrange them in the correct sequence.

Skills:
Progression, sequence, counting

Vocabulary:
Ring, buttons

Materials:
- 10 macrame rings (hobby or handicraft store) 3''–4'' (7.6cm–10.2cm) diameter
- 55 assorted buttons
- 2 containers

Construction:
None

Procedure:
Line the 10 rings horizontally or vertically before you. Place one button in the first ring, two in the second, etc. until all are used. Store the buttons in a small container; put it inside the larger one with the rings.

Number Strips

Level:
Intermediate-Advanced

Objective:
To order the number strips correctly

Skills:
Ordering to reconstruct, ordering to sequence

Vocabulary:
Names of numbers

Materials;
- Wooden yardstick
- Storage container

Construction:
Saw the yardstick into 8 pieces at these points: 1'', 3'', 6'', 10¼'', 15¼'', 21¼'', 28¼''. If the yardstick has numbers on the reverse side, cover them with black marker. Cover advertising to eliminate distraction.

Procedure:
Find the shortest piece and place it lower left on the worksurface as shown. Place the next shortest, and continue until all are used. Use the edge of the table or mat as a guide, if possible. Try a variation: stand the bars vertically to make "steps." Demonstrate graduation as a self-check for both variations.

Number Stick

Level:
Advanced

Objective:
To reassemble the yardstick pieces in order.

Skills:
Number progression, ordering numerically

Vocabulary:
Verbal exchange relating to number recognition.

Materials:
- Wooden yardstick
- Storage container

Construction:
Saw the yardstick every 3 inches on the inch marks. Use the permanent black marker to cover advertising; this eliminates distraction.

Procedure:
Spread the pieces in random order on the worksurface. Find the piece beginning with 1 and join all the pieces to 36. This exercise has many applications in situations in which students are actively learning numbers past ten. Decade, sequence, and pattern can be demonstrated with the help of the yardstick. Use it as you see fit.

Spindle Bar

Level:
Intermediate-Advanced

Objective:
To slip the correct number of sticks under the elastic in each position on the bar.

Skills:
Counting, grouping, associating numbers with objects

Vocabulary:
Sticks, band

Materials:
- 55 colored plastic beverage stirrers or other "spindles"
- An 18" (45.7cm) length of 1" × 2" (2.5cm × 5cm) board
- An 18" (45.7cm) length of elastic, ¾" (19mm) wide
- Heavy-duty staple gun or hammer-in staples
- Container for spindles

Construction:
Stretch the elastic from end to end on the board, centering it, and lapping the ends 1" (2.5cm) on the back. Double staple the ends to the back. Double staple the elastic every 1¾" (4.4cm) on the front of the board to make 10 pockets.

Procedure:
Place one spindle under the band in the #1 position, two in the #2 position, etc. to ten. Numbers may be printed above each position on the bar to simplify the exercise, if needed.

Notes:

Children approach the unknown fearlessly and tenaciously, and their methods are often of the Sherlock Homes school. When they stumble onto answers to their own questions, they mentally pounce on them with shining eyes and a self-satisfied expression that clearly says, "AH-HA!" The Super Sleuth has done it again!

These science exercises are best introduced with a minimum of laboring over scientific concepts which would be lost on young children. Countless students' interest in science has been dampened, if not killed outright, by having to dissect a rose, when what they really wanted to do was smell it. Timing is crucial; "how" and "why" must never precede "what." Uninterrupted observation and reflection are sufficient for now.

Colors

Level:
Intermediate-Advanced

Objective:
To mix primary colors to make secondary ones.

Skills:
Visual discrimination, color responsiveness

Vocabulary:
Conversation pertinent to the exercise

Materials:
- 3 plastic squeeze bottles (honey comes in these; cut a tiny opening in the tip)
- 6 clear plastic cups
- Food color—red, blue, yellow
- 6-cup muffin tin
- Permanent colored markers—red, blue, yellow
- Small spoon

Construction:
Use the markers to make a red dot on the outside of one cup, a blue dot on one, and a yellow dot on one. Make a red and yellow dot on one cup; red and blue on one; and blue and yellow on one. Make halfway marks with black marker on each cup. Brush a coat of waterproof white glue (it will dry clear) or clear nail polish over marks and dots for permanency. Fill each squeeze bottle with water and add food color to make a fairly strong color—10-20 drops, depending on the bottle size.

Procedure:
Use the small pitcher from Clean-up to fill each of the cups with water to the fill mark and put them in the muffin tin to prevent spilling. Use the spoon to put

one (only one) spoonful of the color or colors specified by the dots on the cups in each one. Stir with the spoon, observing the resulting colors. Don't permit aimless "messing" with the colors. If children are unsatisfied at the end of the experience, they should paint a picture or otherwise work with color, or use the WATER activity. They can carry the entire muffin tin to the sink to empty the glasses. Stack the glasses and put all equipment in the tin for storage.

Absorption

Level:
Beginning to Advanced

Objective:
To explore absorption by dipping a sponge in water and squeezing it in order to transfer water from one container to another.

Skills:
Observation of cause and effect, disappearance and reappearance, control of substance

Vocabulary:
Absorb, soak, sponge, squeeze

Materials:
- ½ of a 3'' × 5'' (7.6cm × 12.7cm) cellulose (not polyfoam) sponge
- 2 identical plastic bowls

Construction:
Make fill marks (½ full) on the bowls with permanent marker.

Procedure:
Use the small pitcher from Clean-up to fill one of the bowls to the fill mark. Place the sponge in the water and allow it to absorb as much as it will. Then carefully squeeze it over the other bowl to remove as much water as possible. Transfer all the water in this manner. Repeat as desired. Empty the bowls and clean workspace. Be sure that the sponge is squeezed as dry as possible before putting it away. Stack the bowls and store them with the sponge inside.

Magnification

Level:
Intermediate-Advanced

Objective:
To become familiar with the idea of magnification by viewing objects under a magnifying glass.

Skills:
Exploration, mental cataloging of information

Vocabulary:
Magnify, magnifying glass, bigger, smaller

Materials:
- Small magnifying glass
- Leaves (dried and green), twigs, flowers, fabric, coins, writing sample, magazine picture, shells, pine cone, rocks, etc.
- Container for storage

Construction:
None required.

Procedure:
Examine the materials leisurely, one by one, turning them to see closely. Rotation of 6 or so materials at a time will maintain interest. Encourage students to add to the collection.

Magnetism

Level:
Beginning to Advanced

Objective:
To test objects made of different materials for magnetic attraction.

Skills:
Researching, observation of natural laws, categorizing

Vocabulary:
Magnet, metal, wood, plastic

Materials:
- One or more magnets
- Index card or piece of cardboard
- Button, burned match, paper clip, bottle caps, bolt or nut, nail, wood scrap, eraser, rock, etc.
- Red felt rectangle approximately 6'' × 4½'' (15.2cm × 11.4cm) (¼ of a precut felt rectangle)
- Green felt rectangle approximately 6'' × 4½'' (15.2cm × 11.4cm) (¼ of a precut felt rectangle)
- Storage container

Construction:
None required.

Procedure:
Test each object for attraction and put "yes" ones on the green felt, "no" ones on the red. Encourage children to add found objects to the collection. If more than one magnet is available, they can be used to show positive and negative poles. Place a magnet underneath the card or cardboard and objects on the top to see if magnetic force can pull through another materials. Be sure the storage container is large enough to allow the felt sorters to be laid flat and remind students to put them in first, and the test objects on top.

Scale

Level:
Intermediate-Advanced

Objective:
To experiment with weight and balance

Skills:
Observation of laws of balance, proportion, visual perception

Vocabulary:
Balance, level, weights, beam

Materials:

- An 18'' (45.7cm) length of 1'' × 2'' (2.5cm × 5cm) board
- 2 small plastic containers
- Contact cement or epoxy glue
- Heavy cord—12'' (30.5cm) long
- Screw eye
- S-hook, optional
- Small nuts in the shell
- Storage container for nuts

Construction:

Glue the containers on the ends of the beam. Put the screw eye in the center of the beam. Tie one end of the cord through the screw eye and put the S-hook on the other end, or tie it in a loop. Close the S-hook around the cord with pliers. Try it on the SUSPENSION ROD; if it fails to balance, move the screw eye until it does.

Note: Polyfoam sponges, cut with scissors into eighths, can also be used as weights. If children have trouble balancing nuts, substitute sponge weights, which won't alter the balance as radically as nuts.

Procedure:

Hang the SCALE on one of the center hooks of the SUSPENSION ROD. Put a weight (nut, bean or sponge piece) in one of the cups. What happened to the beam? What can you do to balance it? What must you do to balance it if you put two weights in the cup? Experiment.

Growing Things

This is a grow-your-own-anytime project. Let everybody contribute seeds to the collection. Put them in small bottles, and tape pictures on the outside to identify them, if you wish. Easy-to-grow vegetable seeds, melon seeds, popcorn, dried beans and peas, and birdseed are favorites. A potato chunk that contains an eye will grow potatoes underground, which is a revelation to children. Raw peanuts will do the same.

Place the bottles of seeds on a tray, along with a squeeze bottle for water, and small plastic or paper cups for planting. Hardy seeds will grow in the soil from the school yard, so students can go out and scoop up a cup full, or you may provide a container of potting soil. Show them how deep to plant seeds, to firm the soil over them, and to water carefully with the squeeze bottle to avoid washing them up. Stress the importance of bringing planted cups to an adult who will write the child's name on them with a marker to avoid later disputes and disappointments. Sprouted plants should be put in a window. If they are kept on a tray, it will catch run-off water. Reminders to water plants will be helpful after the novelty has worn off. When the plants are a few inches tall, children can take them home to transplant outdoors, if you like, or they can transplant them into a school garden.

Whisper Tube

Level:
Intermediate-Advanced

Objective:
To whisper into the tube to a friend and observe the carrying of sound.

Skills:
Whispering, observation of sound conduction

Vocabulary:
Whisper, funnel, tube

Materials:
- Clear plastic tubing—6' (1.8m) or longer (hardware store or home center)
- 2 small funnels to fit snugly into the tubing

Construction:
None required.

Procedure:
Fit the funnels into the ends of the tube and whisper and listen with another person. For hearing safety, insist that no sound louder than a whisper be used. Have a whisper session to be sure children know how to whisper. Distinguish it from speaking in a low voice, which children often confuse with whispering. Under no circumstances permit loud play or shouting with the WHISPER TUBE. Ear damage could result. With a very long tube, children can stand out of sight of each other and communicate with the WHISPER TUBE. Hang the tubing over a nail or hook to store; put the funnels on the shelf.

Rocks

Level:
Intermediate-Advanced

Objective:
To pair different kinds of rocks.

Skills:
Visual and tactile discrimination, appreciation of differences, classifying

Vocabulary:
Possibly some of the names of the rocks if known—check a rock and mineral field guide

Materials:
- 10–12 pairs of rocks
- 2 felt rectangles 9'' × 12'' (22.8cm × 30.5cm)
- Small container to hold the rocks
- Large container to hold all

Construction:
For the sorting mats, cut 3'' × 6'' (7.6 cm × 15.2cm) rectangles from the felt, one for each pair of rocks. (If you use precut 9'' × 12'' (22.8cm × 30.5cm) squares, cut them in half crosswise and into thirds lengthwise to make 6.) With a marker and a glass or bottle as a guide, make two circles on each rectangle, approximately 2'' (5cm) in diameter.

Procedure:
Perhaps you know a "rock hound"—someone whose hobby is rock collecting. If so, you are fortunate, because it's a bit difficult to collect enough yard-variety

rocks to make a good exercise. A "rock hound" will be happy to give you chips from many varieties. Try for as varied a collection as possible. You need two pieces of each one, recognizable as a match.

If yard-variety rocks are your only alternative, use them by all means. Crack them with a hammer and some surprisingly interesting colors may appear in even the most mundane-appearing ones.

To match pairs, place them in the circles on the sorting mats. For storage, point out the need to put the rocks in the small container first, to avoid crumpling the mats. Set the container of rocks on the mats in the large container.

Note: SHELLS are a good variation of ROCKS if you happen to have a shell collection. Children love shells. Make the exercise the same way.

Animal Coverings

Level:
Intermediate-Advanced

Objective:
To match pictures of animals with the kind of covering on their bodies.

Skills:
Classification, observation, memory recall

Vocabulary:
Names of all animals used, fur, scales, leather

Materials:
- Animal pictures—3–5 for each kind of covering; you can use children's workbooks as a source
- 3'' (7.6cm) square smooth or short-haired leather sample or fur fabric
- 3'' (7.6cm) long-haired leather sample or fur fabric
- 3'' (7.6cm) square reptile-printed vinyl
- Fish scales
- Feather
- 2 containers for storage

Construction:
Laminate the fish scales (and the feather if it's small) and all the pictures as described under LAMINATING in PUTTING IT ALL TOGETHER.

Procedure:
Arrange the coverings in a horizontal row and place the pictures one by one below them in vertical rows.

You can find leather samples at leather or shoe repair shops, or substitute short-pile and long-pile fur fabric. For fish scales, visit a nearby fish market! Hopefully there are birds in your neighborhood to provide you with at least a small feather. Try a pet shop if not. You may use more than one picture of each kind of animal, if they differ slightly. Here are some examples of each type:

Short hair—horse, cow, pig, elephant
Long hair—dog, cat, monkey, lion
Feather—birds, chicken, turkey, duck
Scales—different kinds of fish
Reptiles—snakes, lizards

Note: This is a beautiful tie-in for zoo and farm trips, and all kinds of animal studies. It has application for art, too. Visual association of animals and how they feel should produce rich paintings. Young children usually don't know fish have scales. Why not bring a fish to school for examination, then use it to make prints? Just brush or roll one side of the fish with easel paint (one or more colors) and press it on a sheet of paper.

Incline

Level:
Intermediate-Advanced

Objective:
To experiment with gravity and with differences in grade by constructing ramps for a marble to roll down.

Skills:
Observation of laws of grade and incline, balance, precision

Vocabulary:
Ramp, slant, risers

Materials:
- 3' (91.4cm) narrow wood cove molding
- 4 polyfoam (not cellulose) sponges
- Marble or small ball
- Storage container

Construction:
Saw the molding into 12'' (30.5cm) lengths. Use scissors to cut the sponges in half cross-wise, then in half again, making fourths, making 16. Only 15 of them are used.

Procedure:
Arrange the ramps in tier fashion, using the sponge risers to form inclines. The arrangement shown uses 5 risers at the highest point, with each stack decreasing by one. Roll the marble from top to bottom. Will it roll if the same number of risers is used at both ends of a ramp? Try and see. Demonstrate the need to elevate one end of the ramp more than the other. A marble is not safe for children who are likely to put it in their mouths. Use a small ball instead. Store the marble or ball separately, if necessary, to prevent its loss.

Bubbles

Level:
Beginning to Advanced

Objective:
To make bubbles with a drinking straw.

Skills:
Experiencing pleasure of creating, observing natural laws, finesse of motion

Vocabulary:
Gently, blow, disappear

Materials:
- Drinking straws
- Shallow pan
- Liquid dishwashing detergent
- Glycerin from a drugstore, optional

Construction:
Mix the bubble solution in these proportions: 1 qt. (.95 l) water, ½ cup (.24 l) liquid detergent. A bit of glycerin will add color and strength to the bubbles. It's important to use the suggested proportion of detergent to water; a weaker solution will make weak bubbles, or none at all. Mix the solution in a gallon jar if possible and pour a small amount in the bubble pan at a time.

Procedure:
Bubbles are fleeting and beautiful and full of wonder! The how or why of them needn't be explained; bubbles can be simply enjoyed. They are capricious, however, and demand care in creation, so teach children the necessity for blowing gently. Children can ask an adult for pre-mixed bubble solution; a half-inch depth of it in the pan is adequate. Drinking straws can be used two ways: dip one end in the solution, lift and blow on the other end, or leave one end in the water and blow, making bubbles in the pan. Discard the drinking straws after use. Children should ask an adult for help to empty the pan when they are finished.

Color Viewers

Level:

Beginning to Advanced

Objective:

To view surroundings through the colored transparencies; to superimpose two of them to make secondary colors from the primary ones.

Skills:

Production of secondary colors, altering view of surroundings

Vocabulary:

Viewers, names of colors (Beginners)

Materials:

- Clear plastic—see LAMINATING in PUTTING IT ALL TOGETHER
- Cellophane tape
- Colored permanent markers in red, blue, yellow
- 3 tongue depressors
- Paper stapler
- Storage container

Construction:

Cut six 4'' (10cm) squares of the plastic. (Mark with ball point pen before cutting.) Trace around an object approximately 3'' (7.6cm) in diameter in the center of three of the squares and color each with a different-colored marker. Place the blank squares on top of the colored ones and seal all edges with cellophane tape. Use a paper stapler to attach them to the tongue depressors, placing the tongue depressors from one corner of the squares to the center. Staple each one 3 times—top, center, and bottom.

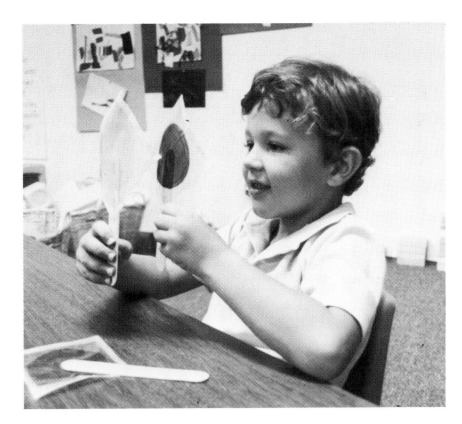

Water

Level:
Beginning to Advanced

Children have a natural affinity for water, as every adult knows—and we go to such great lengths to keep the two separated! Perhaps at no other stage of their development will it hold the fascination it does now—why not take advantage of this? Water experimentation furthers so many skills, it would be difficult to list them all. Suffice it to say it's well worth the risk of a little spilled water!

To keep spilling to a minimum, require users to put the tank on a table; floor use will encourage splashing. Also require them to wear smocks, and to push up long sleeves. Almost any kind of plastic or metal tank or tub will do—even a baby bath. Here are some hints:

1. Children can fill the tank to the fill mark (1/3 full) with the large pitcher from Cleanup.
2. They will need adult help emptying it when they're finished.
3. Remind them that only water equipment may be put in the water.
4. Expect clean-up as part of the activity. (Beginners may need help from adults.)
5. Store water supplies in the empty tank.
6. Rotate 3 or 4 of these at a time: unbreakable cups, bottles, spoons, ladles, sprinklers (or heavy plastic cups with holes punched in the bottom), plastic tubing, funnels, plastic pump bottles, and whatever else you think belongs, as long as it's rustproof.

Musical Pipes

Level:

Beginning to Advanced
(Beginning with
Assistance)

Objective:

To produce musical sounds by striking the metal pipes with the striker.

Skills:

Musical appreciation, manual precision, pitch differentiation

Vocabulary:

Pipes, runners, longest, shortest, striker

Materials:

- Precut metal pipe, ¾'' (19mm) outside diameter, in graduated lengths from 5'' to 12'' (12.7cm to 30.5cm): 5'' (12.7cm), 6'' (15.2cm), 8'' (20cm), 10'' (25.4cm), 12'' (30.5cm)—see Note below.

- 3 polyfoam (not cellulose) sponges

- Contact cement or Wilhold white glue (not Elmer's)

- Long metal bolt

- Tray or other container for storage

Construction:

Use scissors to cut the sponges in half lengthwise. Cut one of the halves in half crosswise, making fourths. Glue two halves and one quarter end to end to make each runner. One half will not be used.

Procedure:

Place the sponge runners on the worksurface in a V shape. Space them the right distance apart, measuring by the longest and shortest pipes. Put the pipes

in place in graduated order. Experiment with sounds by striking lightly with the bolt. Notice that the sound is more bell-like if you hold the striker loosely than if you hold it tightly. Run the striker over the pipes from the longest to the shortest, and reverse. Enjoy.

Note: Precut lengths graduate by 2'' (5cm) up to 12'' (30.5cm); the next length is 24'' (61cm), which is too long for our purposes. Lengths shorter that 5'' (12.7cm) don't produce musical tones, so the set is limited to 5. However, you can have a 24'' (61cm) length cut to 14'' (35.6cm) where you buy it to make a sixth pipe, as I did. Or use a set of five—you'll still have an interesting range of tones.

Bell Sticks

Level:
Intermediate-Advanced

Objective:
To pair the bells according to their sound.

Skills:
Auditory discrimination, concentration, pitch differentiation

Vocabulary:
Jingle, loud, soft

Materials:
- 8 tongue depressors
- 16 jingle bells in 4 different sizes, 4 of each size—handicraft or hobby stores
- 40'' (1.02m) ribbon ¼'' (6mm) wide
- White glue or epoxy
- Storage container

Construction:

Make two identical bell sticks, with each size of bell. Cut the ribbon into 8 strips, each 5'' (12.7cm) long. Thread one strip through two bells of one size. Spread glue on the stick, ½'' (12.7mm) from each end, down the center vertically. Extend the glue beyond all edges of the ribbon to make it secure. Press the ribbon and bells on the glue. Make another identical stick with the other two bells of the same size. Continue with the other sizes of bells.

Procedure:

This is a closed-eyes exercise. A helping friend is nice, to hand the bell sticks to the child performing the exercise, but it can be done alone, too. Mix the sticks randomly on the worksurface, placing them in a horizontal row. Pick up a stick and shake it near your ear. Try another one. Does it sound similar? Shake both sticks at once, one in each hand. What do you think—are they a match? If so, open your eyes to see if the bells are the same size. Place them to the side together if they are, and continue. If the choice was not correct, close your eyes and try another stick, to match the first one you chose.

Flotation

Level:
Beginning to Advanced

Objective:
To test objects made of various materials to see whether they float or sink in water.

Skills:
Experimentation, observation of natural laws, categorizing

Vocabulary:
Float, sink, heavy, light

Materials:

- Small container to hold water

- Twig, leaf, burned match, nail, penny, button, piece of sponge, piece of cardboard, bottle cap, cork, etc.

- 2 felt rectangles approximately 6'' × 4½'' (15.2cm × 11.4cm) (¼ of a precut felt rectangle), one green, one red

- Container to hold all

Construction:

Use a permanent marker to make a fill mark at the halfway point on the water container.

Procedure:

Add water to the container to the fill mark. Test each object and place "yes" ones on the green felt, "no" ones on the red. Encourage children to add found objects to the collection. Empty water. Lay the felt sorters flat in the larger container and put the water container holding the test objects on top of them.

Prism

Level:
Intermediate-Advanced

Objective:
To produce a rainbow with a made-on-the-spot prism.

Skills:
Appreciation of beauty of a rainbow, observation of the way one is made

Vocabulary:
Prism, rays, rainbow, sunbeams

Materials:
- Shallow, unbreakable bowl
- Small hand mirror, *backed with plastic*

Construction:
Make a fill mark on the bowl with permanent marker.

Procedure:
This exercise is for sunny days, because the sun's rays must be striking someplace in the room. Find such a spot, and put the bowl in the sunlight. Bring water in the small pitcher from Cleanup to pour into the bowl to the fill mark. Discourage carrying water in the bowl—it's too shallow. Place the mirror in the water, submerging the glass completely. Adjust by tilting it against the bowl's edge until a rainbow appears on the wall or ceiling or a piece of white paper. Prisms are fun—why they work is not important for now—the fact that they do is. The bowl can be the storage container for the mirror. If this presents a safety hazard for your group, store the mirror separately and have students ask for it to do the exercise. Observe necessary precautions to assure that it is used with care.

Time

A hand-set timer can be an important piece of classroom equipment for everybody's use. Give it a permanent spot and invite intermediate and advanced students and staff to use it, *but not to move it.* Students can set it to mark "turns" taken with a toy or piece of equipment. This should be on their own initiative, however: adults should not become involved with their turn-taking. Children devise different ways to share things equitably, and this can be a convenient way of doing it while developing time awareness at the same time. The timer represents an impartial third party which will be respected by all. It can settle numerous disputes.

Notes:

Life Arts

If there is a heart to an individualized classroom, it must be the LIFE ARTS section. It's here that children lose themselves in physical activities when their spirits say, "No more!" to further mental exertion. These simple activities are relaxing; they have the comfort of the familiar.

Moving children toward independence is the ultimate goal of all education—helping them to help themselves. This may include learning to pour one's own milk, as well as mastery of academic skills. Performing everyday tasks using tools and utensils they see being used in their homes is the whole idea behind LIFE ARTS. And why not? I can't think of one good reason why they shouldn't be allowed—invited!—to use such a fascinating gadget as an eggbeater! (Can you think of a better exercise in eye-hand coordination?)

A Note About Life Arts

What is the knowledge of how an eggbeater works worth in practical terms? Not much. It would certainly rate low on a list of basic life skills. Ah, but mastery! Competence! An "I can do it!" assurance—the more often children experience these, the better their chances for success with whatever else they attempt. Whatever strengthens self-confidence has far-reaching consequences.

Clean-up equipment will be used more frequently with LIFE ARTS activities than with the others, because of the nature of the activities. Control of materials and substances will come with time. Only in cases of deliberate or excessively careless mishandling should use of the exercises be restricted, because the children who need them most are the ones who can control them least. A teacher's relaxed, accepting attitude will hasten the day the entire class can perform them easily and well.

CUTTING, SLICING, and SANDWICHES are such favorites that keeping the ingredients on hand for them becomes too expensive for most schools if they are used every day. Two or three times weekly is adequate. Food in their containers on the shelf signals that the exercises may be used. GINGERBREAD is an extra-special activity which can be done monthly or so. Non-food activities can be used daily.

Tongs

Level:
Intermediate–Advanced

Objective:
To sort the nuts using tongs.

Skills:
Eye-hand coordination, precision, sorting

Vocabulary:
Tongs, names of the nuts used

Materials:
- Tongs
- 4 small unbreakable bowls
- 15 nuts in the shell—3 kinds, 5 of each kind
- Small tray for storage

Procedure:
Encourage students to try to use only the tongs and not fingers to sort the nuts. However, they may use either to replace the nuts in the holding container after they have finished the exercise. Arrange the bowls on the tray or worksurface. Transfer the nuts, one at a time. Repeat by transferring them all back into the holding bowl if desired. Changing the kinds of nuts used occasionally will help maintain interest and alter the experience slightly.

Spatula

Level:
Beginning to Advanced

Objective:
To transfer the sponge pieces from the table to the tray with the spatula.

Skills:
Steadiness, using tool as extension of hand

Vocabulary:
Lift, sponge, layer

Materials:
- Spatula
- Small tray
- 4 polyfoam (not cellulose) sponges, cut with scissors into fourths

Procedure:
Place the sponge pieces on the worksurface in random order. Use the spatula to lift them one at a time and place them on the try, arranging them in rows. One layer is enough for Beginners; Intermediates and Advanced may add a second layer, placing the pieces evenly on top of the first layer. If the sponges are in mixed colors, children often sort them by color as they transfer them. Encourage them to repeat the exercise to their satisfaction. Everything can be stored on the tray.

Tweezers

Level:
  Intermediate–Advanced

Objective:
  To transfer the beads using only tweezers, from the holding container to the other three, sorting them in the process.

Skills:
  Eye-hand coordination, precision, control of movement

Vocabulary:
  Tweezers, beads

Materials:
  - 12 to 18 small beads in three different colors or designs
  - Tweezers
  - Four small unbreakable bowls
  - Small tray

Procedure:
  Leave the bowls on the tray or put them on the worksurface in a convenient arrangement. Use the tweezers to transfer the beads one by one from the holding bowl to the other three, sorting them at the same time. Repeat if desired. The beads should be put into the holding bowl at the end of the exercise.

  Note: This exercise is not safe for use with children of any age who are likely to put the beads in their mouths.

Sifter

Level:
Intermediate–Advanced

Objective:
To sift cornmeal with the sifter.

Skills:
Care in handling, eye-hand coordination, precision

Vocabulary:
Sift, sifter

Materials:
- Sifter, small or large—check for ease of operation
- Cornmeal, approximately 1 cupful (236ml)
- 2 identical medium-to-large unbreakable bowls
- Tablespoon

Procedure:
Moderately good control is required to prevent scattering the cornmeal but most children can manage if they work slowly and carefully. Demonstrate deliberate movements and repeat an individual lesson for everyone who has trouble. Hold the sifter over the empty bowl while using the spoon to dip the cornmeal from the other bowl into the sifter. Sift slowly into the bowl, and repeat as desired.

Important: Point out that the sifter must be held over one of the bowls as it's being filled, not over the table. Demonstrate cleanup. The whiskbroom will clean the cornmeal from the floor with less scattering than the broom. Store the cornmeal separately if necessary. Store the sifter in the stacked bowls.

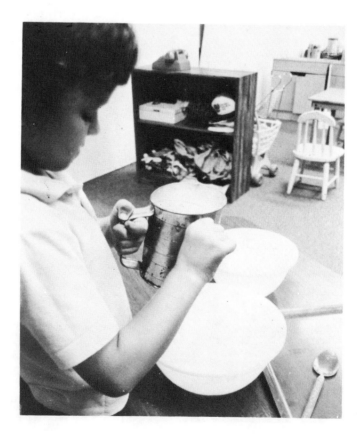

Beater

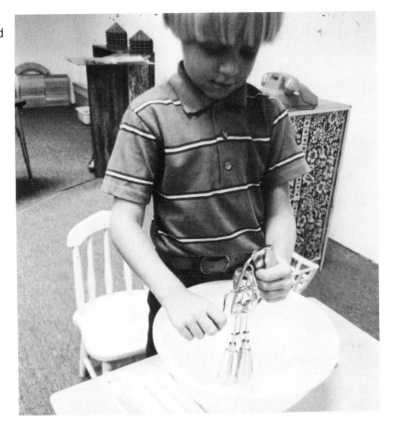

Objective:
To use an eggbeater to make soapsuds.

Skills:
Altering a substance, control of water, control of utensil.

Vocabulary:
Eggbeater, suds

Materials:
- Rotary eggbeater—check for ease of operation
- Unbreakable, large, deep bowl
- Dishwashing liquid

Procedure:
Place a folded towel from Cleanup under the bowl to prevent slipping. Fill the bowl to the fill mark (¼ full) with the pitcher from Cleanup, and take it to an adult for a squeeze of dishwashing liquid. Show how to hold the eggbeater vertically and turn it smoothly until the bowl is filled with suds. Demonstrate cleanup: empty the bowl in the sink, dry it with the towel, dry the table if necessary and put the towel in the hamper. Store the beater in the bowl.

Pitcher

Level:
Intermediate–Advanced

Objective:
To pour water from a pitcher into glasses.

Skills:
Pouring technique, control of substance and utensils, visual/spatial consciousness

Vocabulary:
Pitcher, overflow

Materials:
- Very small pitcher or measuring cup with a spout
- 2 very small clear plastic glasses or cups
- Small tray

Procedure:
Learning to pour liquids involves more complex motions than adults realize, but if the steps are broken down, young children can learn them easily. They often make the mistake of tilting the cup as it's being filled, inviting a spill, or they unbalance the act by bringing the cup up to the pitcher. When they learn to keep the cup on the table, both problems are solved.

Put water in the small pitcher at the tap (or ask an adult). Hold it in the "crayon hand" (the dominant hand). This is important, because children often attempt to hold the cup, instead of the pitcher, in their dominant hand. Hold the cup with the other hand, keeping it flat on the table. Pour slowly, watching to stop well before an overflow occurs. Repeat with the other cup. Pour both cups of water back into the pitcher and repeat as many times as desired. Demonstrate cleanup.

Remind children this water is not for drinking (the cups are not sanitary), but for pouring.

Note: Be sure the cups are clear, not opaque, so the level of the water can be easily seen.

Scoop

Level:
  Beginning to Advanced

Objective:
  To scoop popcorn to fill the sections of the ice cube tray.

Skills:
  Control of materials, fine muscle control

Vocabulary:
  Popcorn, scoop

Materials:
  - Plastic dishpan or other large container
  - Unpopped popcorn to fill dishpan ¼ full
  - Small scoop
  - Plastic ice cube tray or 6-cup muffin tin
  - Medium-sized tray

Procedure:
  Set the ice cube tray on the tray beside the dishpan of popcorn or hold it above the dishpan. Scoop slowly and carefully to fill each section of the ice cube tray, spilling as little popcorn as possible. Carefully pour the ice cube tray of popcorn back in the dishpan and repeat as desired. Empty popcorn from the catching tray back into the dishpan at the end of the exercise, and store it underneath or on top of the dishpan. The ice cube tray can be stored in the dishpan.

  Note: Use this activity with Beginners with adult supervision only—not at all if the children put foreign objects in their mouths.

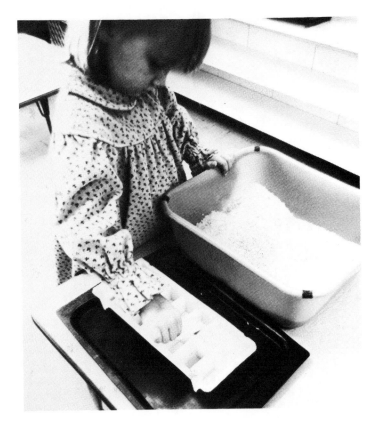

Measures

Level:
Beginning to Advanced

Objective:
To measure dried beans with cups and spoons.

Skills:
Measuring, observation of volume, enjoyment of motions

Vocabulary:
Names of the different kinds of beans

Materials:
- Plastic dishpan
- 1 set of measuring cups
- 1 set of measuring spoons
- Dried beans to fill dishpan ¼ full

Procedure:
Choose any kind of beans, or several different kinds. Different-sized ones fill the measures differently—more small ones are needed to fill a cup than large ones—so there is some advantage to using different sizes separately and rotating them.

It's best to let students discover for themselves that the cups and spoons are all multiples. Remind them of the need to keep the measuring containers over the dishpan while they're filling them. Cups and spoons may be stored in the pan with the beans.

Note: Use this activity for Beginners with adult supervision only—not at all if they are likely to put the beans in their mouths. Use only large beans with Beginners.

Slicing

Level:
Intermediate–Advanced

Objective:
To cut carrot slices with a table knife and share them with classmates.

Skills:
Sense of accomplishment, social interaction, proficiency with a knife

Vocabulary:
Cutting board, serve, rinse

Materials:
- Small carrot in a plastic sandwich bag
- Small cutting board (a lumber scrap will do)
- Medium-sized unbreakable bowl
- Small vegetable brush
- Table knife
- Small unbreakable plate or saucer
- Tray to hold all

Procedure:
Wash hands. Put water in the bowl to the fill mark (halfway). Brush and wash the carrot thoroughly. Hold the knife in the dominant hand and the carrot with the other, on the cutting board. Make even crosswise slices, ½" thick or so, starting on the end furthest from the hand holding the carrot. Slice slowly and carefully. (A serrated vegetable cutter may be used by advanced students; it's a bit more difficult but makes interesting-looking slices.) Place the slices on the plate. Clean the workspace *before* serving classmates. Store the knife separately if you think it advisable.

Remind children to allow others to take their own carrot slices from the plate. "Would you like a carrot slice?" is a good way to ask. One to a customer, and an answer of "No" is acceptable. (Thank you's are appreciated but optional—better sincere or absent than forced.)

There won't be enough slices to serve the entire class, but the exercise is repeated often, so those who don't have one this time will the next.

Cutting

Level:
Intermediate–Advanced

Objective:
To cut a slice of bread into fourths and share it.

Skills:
Sense of accomplishment, social interaction, respect for knife

Vocabulary:
Slice, serve

Materials:
- Small cutting board (a lumber scrap will do)
- Table knife
- Small unbreakable plate or saucer
- Slice of bread in a sandwich bag
- Tray to hold all

Procedure:
Wash hands. Hold the knife in the dominant hand and use the other hand to hold the bread on the cutting board. Emphasize gentle, sawing motions to avoid tearing the bread. Firm-sliced (or less-than-fresh) bread works best. Cut it in half *from top to bottom* first, then cut each in half across. Put the four squares on the plate. Clean the workspace *before* serving to three or four others in the class. Remind children to let others take a piece for themselves. See more notes on serving in the SLICING exercise. Store the knife separately it you think it advisable.

Towel Washing

Level:
Intermediate–Advanced

Objective:
To wash the towels used for Cleanup.

Skills:
Control of substance, familiarity with laundry process, responsibility for actions, follow through

Vocabulary:
Scrub, scrub board, squeeze, rinse

Materials:
- Plastic dishpan
- Small scrub board
- Bar of soap
- Small folding drying rack or clothesline

Procedure:
Collect the towels from the hamper. Fill the dishpan to the fill mark (1/3 full) using the large pitcher from Cleanup. Children shouldn't attempt to fill the dishpan at the tap and carry it to the table. Put a clean folded towel underneath the dishpan if it moves on the table. Wet each towel, spread it on the rubbing surface of the scrub board and rub the bar of soap on it. Scrub on the board and rinse. Squeeze (children can't wring) as dry as possible. Emphasize the need to squeeze well to prevent puddles under the drying rack. Spread and smooth the towels on the drying rack or clothesline, draping in half. Ask an

adult for help to empty the water, if necessary, and dry the table. The soap and scrub board are stored in the dishpan.

Note: Clean towels are not the only goal of this activity. They could be machine-laundered (as they should be occasionally), or paper towels could be used, but that would be a missed opportunity for children to learn through their hands. Even though, in this country, clothes are not routinely washed by hand, agitation and rinsing are essentially the same whether it's done by hand or machine. What happens in automatic washers and dryers is a mystery to children. They see clothes go in the washer dry and come out wet, and go in the dryer wet and come out dry. Somehow they end up clean. Well, now they can see what really happens, and the activity is one of their favorites.

Towel Folding

Level:
   Intermediate–Advanced

Objective:
   To fold the dried towels and replace them on the shelf. (Not necessarily done by the one who washed them.)

Skills:
   Observation of final step of laundry process, observation of cycles, manual precision, visual judgment

Vocabulary:
   Crease, fold

Materials:
   • The clean dried towels on the drying rack or clothesline

Procedure:
   The towels are folded in quarters. Show that corners are matched on both the first and second folds, and the crease smoothed with the hands. Place the stack of folded towels on the shelf with the cleanup supplies.

Sandwiches

Objective:
To prepare a small snack and share it with a friend. (This is a culmination of the CUTTING and TABLE SETTING exercises.)

Skills:
Responsibility for an extended activity, carrying out sequential steps, reward of enjoying results of labor, follow-through, cooperation

Vocabulary:
Table setting, wash, dry, slice, spread, place mat

Materials:
- 2 small plastic place mats (a regular-sized one cut in half)
- 2 small clear plastic cups (disposable if desired)
- 3 small unbreakable plates or saucers
- Table knife
- Paper napkins (regular-sized ones cut in half or fourths)
- Small pitcher
- Small capped container holding a small amount of peanut butter
- Bread slice in a sandwich bag
- Tray to hold all

These cleanup supplies will be needed afterwards (store on the shelf with the above materials):

- 2 plastic dishpans—one for washing, one for rinsing
- Sponge to be used for this exercise only (½ of a full-sized one)
- Small dish drain rack (a towel may be used instead)

Procedure:

Show the entire activity, step by step, including washing and putting away dishes. Ask another adult to play the part of the second child if possible. The child who chose the activity prepares the snack and asks a friend to share it; both share cleanup. This is the order:

1. Wash hands
2. Make sandwiches: (1) cut the bread in fouths; (2) spread two pieces thinly with peanut butter and put top pieces on; (3) put sandwiches on a plate
3. Put water in the pitcher, or ask an adult
4. Set the table
5. Ask a friend to join you
6. Each pours and serves self
7. Put water in dishpans with pitcher from Cleanup or ask an adult
8. Ask adult for a squeeze of liquid dishwashing detergent for one dishpan
9. One washes dishes, one dries and replaces them on the tray on the shelf
10. Empty dishpan, dry table, put away supplies

Note: Dishes, especially the cups, if they are not disposable, should be rewashed by adults and sterilized.

Gingerbread

Intermediate—Advanced:

Cooking and children are a marvelous combination. Measuring, stirring, observing ingredients change as they're combined and as they're cooked—it's a mini-course in science and math!

Making gingerbread requires one-to-one assistance from an adult, but the roles of the child and adult should remain clear: the child is the cook, the adult the assistant.

Whenever the supplies and ingredients are placed on the shelf, a child may ask an adult for help to make gingerbread. It's made only once on that day. A written record of bakers is a good idea; no repeats until all who wish have had an opportunity.

None of the ingredients need refrigeration, in case your school has no refrigerator. If you haven't an oven either, a portable toaster oven can be used.

This recipe will make enough gingerbread for each child in an average-sized class to have a tiny piece. Help the cook to cut it into enough pieces to serve everyone.

The cooking utensils are not washed by the child; an adult should wash them after class so they will be cleaned thoroughly.

Following the recipe given, make a picture recipe that children can follow without reading. List the ingredients and beside each one draw cups and spoons and label them with the appropriate measurements. For example, beside the word "flour" draw 2 full-size cups and one half-cup; write the number *one* in the two full cups and the fraction *one-half* in the half-cup, to indicate that two and one-half cups of flour are used.

Laminate the recipe according to the directions in LAMINATING, in PUTTING IT ALL TOGETHER. Label the containers holding the ingredients with a permanent marker. Write the measurements on the measuring cups and spoons with permanent marker so they will correspond with the ones in the picture recipe, and be easy to read. Brush a coat of waterproof white glue (it will dry clear) or clear nail polish over all markings for permanency.

Gingerbread Recipe

2½ cups flour
¼ teaspoon salt
1½ teaspoons soda
2 teaspoons pumpkin pie spice, or equal parts cinnamon, ginger, and cloves
1 cup molasses
½ cup oil
1 cup water

Bake at 350 degrees for 30–35 minutes.

Assemble in two dishpans, one for ingredients, one for equipment:

Ingredients:
1. Flour—in a covered container
2. Molasses—in a squeeze bottle
3. Baking soda—in a small covered container
4. Salt—in a small covered container
5. Vegetable oil—in a squeeze bottle
6. Pumpkin pie spice (or equal parts cinnamon, ginger, and cloves combined)—in a small covered container.

Equipment:
1. Dry measuring cups—1 cup (236ml) and ½ cup (118ml)
2. Liquid measuring cup
3. Measuring spoons—1 teaspoon (33ml), ½ teaspoon (16ml), ¼ teaspoon (1.2ml)
4. Mixing spoon
5. Medium-to-large unbreakable mixing bowl
6. Baking pan, approximately 8''×8'' (20cm×20cm)
7. Table knife and spatula
8. Sifter
9. Small tray or unbreakable plate

Procedure:
1. Wash hands.
2. Bring both dishpans to a table.
3. Set the sifter in the mixing bowl.
4. Measure the dry ingredients into it and sift into the bowl.
5. Add the liquid ingredients and stir thoroughly.
6. Pour into the baking pan and bake. (It's not necessary to oil the pan.)
7. Set a timer for the baking time if one is available.
8. Clean workspace, put ingredients back on the shelf. (Adult removes used utensils.)
9. An adult removes the cooked gingerbread from the oven.
10. Cut the cooled gingerbread into small squares, with an adult's help.
11. Put the squares on tray or plate with the spatula and serve classmates and staff.

Table Setting

Level:
Beginning to Advanced

Objective:
To place the plastic tableware in the positions on the mats as indicated by the outlines on one mat.

Skills:
Recognition of differences, sorting, organizing, duplicating a pattern

Vocabulary:
Fork, knife, spoon, plate, napkin, cup

Materials:
- 4 unbreakable saucers
- 4 small unbreakable cups or glasses
- Plastic flatware—heavyweight—4 each forks, spoons, knives
- 4 pieces of felt 9'' × 12'' (22.8cm × 30.5cm) in one color
- 4 pieces of felt 4'' × 4'' (10 cm × 10cm) in a second color
- Silverware tray for storage

Construction:
Use the black marker to trace around a saucer in the center of one mat; trace around a cup at its upper right; trace around a fork on the left of it and a knife and spoon on the right. Fold a 4'' × 4'' (10cm × 10cm) piece of paper diagonally and trace around it inside the saucer outline to represent a folded napkin. For Beginners, make outlines on all mats.

Procedure:

Arrange the place mats on the worksurface. Complete the place settings on the outlined mat by placing a saucer, fork, spoon, cup and knife on the outlines. Fold one of the small felt squares in half diagonally (point out the need to match corners) and place it in the saucer on the mat. Repeat the pattern by placing the other pieces on the remaining mats. Store the dishes and flatware in the silverware tray, and set it on top of the mats and napkins.

Note: For very young Beginners, make outlines on all four mats (or use only two). Place tableware directly on the outlines.

Strainer

Level:
Intermediate–Advanced

Objective:
To observe the function of a sieve to separate large and small particles.

Skills:
Fine muscle control, observation of gradation

Vocabulary:
Strain, sieve, gravel, pebbles

Materials:
- Plastic dishpan
- Fine sand to fill the container ¼ full
- Gravel or pebbles
- Small container to hold gravel
- Large-mesh strainer (sieve)

Procedure:
Dip the strainer to fill with sand and gravel or fill it with the hands. Shake it gently from side to side, not up and down, to make the sand fall through the mesh. Observe what happens to the gravel. Pour the collected gravel into the small container. Continue until satisfied with the amount of gravel collected, then empty it back into the sand before putting it away. Everything may be stored in the dishpan.

Dropper

Level:
Intermediate–Advanced

Objective:
To use a medicine dropper to transfer water from one cup to another.

Skills:
Fine muscle control, control of substance, eye-hand coordination

Vocabulary:
Suction, medicine dropper, squeeze

Materials:
- Plastic medicine dropper (drugstore)
- 2 small clear plastic cups
- Food color
- Small tray

Procedure:
Leave the cups on the tray or put them on the table. Fill one cup to the fill mark (½ full) and ask an adult to add food color. Show how dropper works: the tricky part is drawing the water into the tube; the bulb must be compressed while the tip is in the water and released before lifting it out. Releasing the water is easier: hold the dropper over the other cup and compress the bulb. Demonstrate this several times, slowly. Try to transfer all of the water from one cup to the other and repeat as desired. Discard the water at the end of the exercise.

Note: Colored water makes for easy viewing. If you transfer one-ounce bottles of food color to dropper bottles from a drugstore, it will be easy to add a drop or two to the water.

Baster

Objective:
To transfer the water from one cup to the other with the baster.

Skills:
Control of utensil, control of substance, eye-hand coordination

Vocabulary:
Baster, squeeze, suction

Materials:
- Kitchen baster
- 2 large clear plastic cups
- Small tray

Procedure:
Keep the cups on the tray during use, or put them on the table. Fill one to the fill mark (½ full) with water and ask an adult for food color. The principle for transferring the water is the same as for DROPPER; hold the tip in the water, squeeze the bulb and release it to draw water into the tube; transfer it to the other cup and release. Try to empty the first cup completely and repeat as desired. Discard the water at the end of the exercise.

Note: Colored water makes for easy viewing. If you transfer one-ounce bottles of food color to dropper bottles from a drugstore, it will be easy to add a drop or two to the water.

Funnel

Level:

Beginning to Advanced

Objective:

To observe the function of a funnel by using one to fill a bottle with rice.

Skills:

Observations of quantity and volume, control of materials, manual dexterity

Vocabulary:

Rice, funnel

Materials:

- Plastic dishpan or other large container
- Rice to fill the dishpan ¼ full
- Narrow-mouthed plastic bottles
- Funnel
- Ladle or large spoon
- Medium-sized tray

Procedure:

A funnel facilitates filling a small-mouthed container. For our purposes, it's also a good coordination activity and fun to do as well. Hold the bottle over the dishpan or set it in on the tray, put the funnel in it, and dip rice into the funnel. Empty and refill as long as desired. Empty rice from the tray back into the dishpan at the end of the exercise. Store the bottles and spoon in the dishpan, and store the tray underneath.

Note: Use this activity with Beginners with adult supervision only—not at all if the children put foreign objects in their mouths.

Food Preparation

Intermediate—Advanced:

A bowl of potatoes and a vegetable peeler are an open invitation that most children find irresistible. So is a bowl of fresh green beans or peas in the shell. Just demonstrate the correct way to use a peeler; it's quite safe. Show how to break green beans into pieces, and how to shell peas when some are available. Allow children to do only a few, if interest lags, and return the rest to the shelf for someone else. Or they may finish them all if they want. Add a few ingredients and make soup for everyone to share.

Why Stop Here?

Individualize Snack Time......Why Not?

If children are over-eager for breaks such as outside play and snacks, it may indicate that they're not receiving sufficient stimulation from class activities. It is possible for them to become so engrossed in what they are doing that they resent being interrupted for anything. Children who are challenged by absorbing activities often treat snacks so casually that they sometimes skip them altogether. If a snack has lost its appeal as reward or relief it becomes what it really is—a refreshment for those who feel the need of it. At this point, rather than interrupt individuals who are busy, the logical step may be to individualize snack time, too. Some schools put snacks at the children's disposal and allow those who wish to help themselves, one at a time, over a period of perhaps an hour. You should expect a rush at the snack table at first. Minor skirmishes are best worked out by the ones involved; it will be temporary. You'll need small tables, two or more for a large class, or a designated space on a large table, a plate containing the snack food and a small pitcher of the beverage, if any. Place cups and napkins on the table, and a wastebasket nearby. You could pour cups of the beverage beforehand, but then an opportunity would be missed for children to do for themselves. If they have worked with the PITCHER exercise, even three-year-olds can usually handle the pitcher if it's small. Individualized snacks are not appropriate for children under age three, and some classes of threes may not be ready.

Have a standing rule that each child take one piece of the snack food (or whatever amount you specify), or better yet, place a small sign reading 1,2,3, or 4 on the table and cut the snack food into pieces beforehand to allow each child to count out his portion. Begin with foods cut into one or two pieces, and add three and four later.

A child having a snack should remain seated the entire time, and leave the snack table clean. This is a must. The occasional incidence of a child being carried away with the freedom to help herself can be handled effectively by having an adult serve her until she is able to do it for herself, and self-control will usually follow. If clean-up is consistently neglected, follow the same procedure: an adult should serve and clean up after the child until he or she is ready to try again.

What About Lunch Time?

In an extended-day school, lunch is one of the most important opportunities to share time in the school day. Every teacher owes a calm and refreshing lunch time to himself and his students. It really is possible! Let children do what they do best —use their own hands to help serve. You might consider allowing them to take their own bread and/or dessert from trays carried by other children, utilizing the skills they have learned from LIFE ARTS exercises. They will be expert with spatulas, spoons, and tongs after working with them. In fact, children can serve themselves or each other any part of lunch as long as the dishes are not hot. After-lunch clean-up can be a team effort, too, and of course table-setting is a good way for them to use their hands.

Notes:

Construction

Initiative begins at birth. A newborn practices it with his first cry. It brings a response; he made something happen. For the rest of his life, the human being will experience a gentle tug-of-war between following and initiating; when to be cooperative, when to be assertive? Personality will suffer if an imbalance occurs in either direction. Through children's early years, we adults may overemphasize cooperation—compliant children are a convenience to us. But by recognizing and supporting their inborn drive to create—to "make things"—we can help right the balance.

Individualized learning activities are inherently weighted toward following. The same singular function that makes them effective as learning tools also rules out user initiative. They are about reacting—their purpose is to evoke reaction. But what of action? How do children learn to start, control production, and follow through—*to make something happen?* They do it by changing things, by reinventing what has already been invented. They do it by making things—their own things, their own way.

A Note About Construction

The soul of an individualized classroom is the CONSTRUCTION area. Children find themselves here. It's where they are most masterful and least self-conscious.

If that sounds impassioned, I'm afraid it is—the CONSTRUCTION area is my favorite part of the classroom, and I'm going to do my best to make you feel the same way! I intend to uncomplicate child art—take the scare right out of it. You, the adult, only have to be responsible for three things: space, time and materials. Children will supply the difficult part—inspiration and labor. They're eager to!

It's too bad we have come to believe child art must be mystical, or at least novel, or, worse yet, cute. Nonsense! It needs to be real—really the child's! All we have to do is provide the means and stand back. They'll provide the ways.

Have you heard the lines, "Give me a fish and I will eat for a day; teach me to fish and I will eat for a lifetime"? They express the concept behind an individualized art program perfectly. Under a teacher's direction (and possibly with her precut patterns) children can produce clever copies of somebody else's ideas, all exactly alike. This is giving them a fish. Their creativity is being defined and limited by someone else. Why not teach them to fish for themselves? Children who know they can succeed at pleasing themselves by executing and carrying out their own plans come to know they can succeed in other ways, too.

As for group art projects, you'll want to continue them along with individualized art. Cooperative efforts, such as murals, can't be replaced. Neither can many other art projects which are not suited to individualization. Continue all these, but expect to find the best art done by children working in the CONSTRUCTION area on their own.

A teacher's responsibilities for the program are not complicated; the first two, time and space, can be scheduled easily. The third one, providing materials, requires a bit more planning. They are not passed out a sheet of paper and a few crayons at a time. They are all there, all the time. Accessibility is the key, and the supplies have to be generous, constant, and varied—children are big consumers. Don't let that worry you, though; discards and basic art supplies are all that you will need.

After your CONSTRUCTION area becomes the busy beehive you are aiming for, you'll still need to be alert to keep it organized and well-supplied. Your behind-the-scenes preparation will keep it working.

Creations sometimes become so prolific that keeping the area uncluttered is a problem. Without discouraging creativity, the CONSTRUCTION area must be kept organized in its own best interest. It will take on a shopworn appearance without diligent attention from the staff. Don't let it become a catchall for half-finished projects and don't tolerate scattered supplies or materials which have been carelessly returned to the shelves. Creativity is not license to disorderliness. Expect and insist on the same respect for materials here as in the rest of the classroom. Dwindling supplies and lost tools will spell the end of a once-viable CONSTRUCTION area.

Construction for Beginners

Beginners (age 2½–3) are limited in their ability to use art materials independently. A suitable program for them is easy to devise, though; their creative needs are fairly simple. They need much repetition of the basic skills which will become further refined as they develop. They need the opportunity to become acquainted with tools and media by using them over and over. Producing something is not the point—becoming comfortable with materials and enjoying the processes is.

Scissors, crayons, paper, paint, and glue are the basic supplies. Scissors are difficult for beginners. Cutting strips into squares is a major achievement for them. (See the PAPER STRIPS exercise) Gluing something onto paper is another challenge. Gluing all kinds of collage materials onto a backing, with an adult's help, can be repeated many times with no loss of interest. Crayons and paint (with supervison), used on large sheets of paper, acquaint the muscles with control of substances, and should be used freely and often. No suggestions of "what to make" should be given. They will concentrate on the materials themselves, putting them on the paper, and their own sensations, which are enough. Let them work uninterrputed.

Of course, beginners can't do even these activities independently and individually. Work with very small groups, or one-to-one. Keep sessions short, but frequent.

Collage

Level:

Intermediate to
Advanced

Collage making is often the core of preschool art, and for good reason. On the one hand, it's a non-threatening activity for children who are unsure of their creative abilities. After all, there's no one "right" way to make a collage. On the other hand, it's a perfect outlet for those children who are ready for the challenge which composition presents. For them, the opportunity for conscious arrangement, under their own direction, is what matters.

Collage deserves its own table, as an ever-ready invitation to paticipate. It will be used most of the time. If you have a small circular table, that's perfect. If not, any other shape in a small size will do. A half-sheet of plywood, as mentioned in *ROOM ARRANGEMENT,* will make a 4' x 4' (122cm x 122cm) square table, which works quite well. Use tape to divide it into fourths to limit the number of participants if necessary.

A cat litter tray can be used to hold the collage materials if the table is large enough; a large tray if it's not. It is set in the center of the table, along with a small container holding scissors. Be sure these are not the same ones for general use, or they'll never be here when needed. Mark the collage scissors with tape, to make sure they stay put. Juice cans of glue made from the recipe in this section or paste with brushes will be added by an adult when the table is in use.

Small items such as bottle caps, etc. should have their own containers on the collage tray. Backing materials, such as construction paper, shirt cardboards, aluminum frozen dinner trays, and styrofoam trays are nearby on the shelf. No suggestions are given for design, though you may vary the composition sometimes by having an "outdoor" tray—leaves, twigs, found scraps of paper, etc. (students will obligingly collect these), or a "red" tray, or a "square" tray, and so on. A request for discards to parents will usually keep you a good supply. Here are possibilities:

Buttons, fabric scraps	Feathers, leaves, seeds
Laces, trims, spools, etc.	Colored tissue, crepe paper, gift
Bottle caps	wrapping
Plastic egg carton sections	Tiny boxes
Pipe cleaners	Styrofoam packaging materials, all
Pasta, all shapes	shapes
Toothpicks	Wood shavings
Photography and computer discards	Old jewelry, beads, etc.
String, yarn, wire, ribbon	Dried seeds, popcorn
Paper scraps	

Pockets

When my sons were younger, pockets were in evidence all around our house for a few years. I taught them to make paper pockets with glue or staples when they were preschool age. They were envelopes, really, made in all sizes. My sons used them to hold pictures and school papers, and sometimes they made them into envelopes for homemade birthday cards and Valentines. Later we graduated to fabric scraps and needles and thread. These cloth pockets were used for all kinds of things—bags for toys and other treasures, sleeping bags for toy animals (and our pet gerbil), and other things I admired at the time and have since forgotten. When they were in junior high school, I taught them to use my sewing machine, and in addition to mending their own shirts and shorts now and then, they made more pockets! But this time they turned into baseball bases and backpacks.

Teach your students how to make pockets by showing them how to fold a piece of paper in half (match corners carefully) and crease. Then glue or staple two sides closed and you have a pocket. Try it and see what inventive uses they devise for them. Make fabric ones too: staple them closed and show how to cut vertical slits around the top edge so they can run a yarn drawstring through to make a bag that closes. Young children can't cut rectangles accurately enough to make the sides match; they need precut rectangles of paper and cloth in different sizes.

Puppets

Here are three easily-made puppets to start ideas flowing, but I hope your students' dramatic presentations won't be limited to them. A puppet can be anything a child gives life to; add a theatre which is quick and easy for children to set up and delightfully spontaneous productions are sure to follow.

Don't be surprised if spur-of-the-moment shows have a cast or an audience of *one,* and a script that is equally abbreviated. Lavish productions with bonafide rehearsals are for a later stage of development. For now it is enough for children to speak through puppets and allow puppets to speak for them.

At this stage, teachers can best assure uninhibited, natural performance by re-maining relatively uninvolved, unless asked directly for help. Even though the dialogue and characterization of child-produced shows may lack finesse, children are usually appreciative of each other's efforts and that's what matters most. In this case, adults are wise to stay discreetly in the background to allow artistry to flower.

Many of these puppets will never get onstage, but they're fun for the making. Show a few children how to make them and they can share the information. If your discard collection is abundant, children will embellish the puppets endlessly, adding jewelry and accessories of all kinds to make them true "characters."

1. *Stick Puppet*—start with two tongue depressors or pop sticks stapled, taped, or tied, in a cross, with the cross-stick nearer one end of the first stick than the other—this will be the arms. Staple or glue a paper or fabric head and "clothes" to the front side of the cross, leaving 2" (5.08cm) at the bottom to hold. Make facial features with crayon or markers and glue on yarn hair if desired.

2. *Tube Puppet*—make a crumpled newspaper head and push it slightly into one end of a cardboard tube from bathroom tissue. Drape a fabric square that is ap-proximately 14" (35.6cm) over the head, allowing it to fall down over the tube

 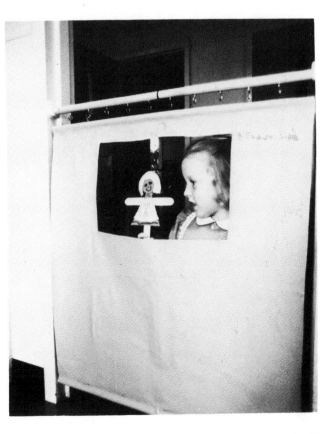

and tie yarn around the "neck." Add yard hair and facial features with markers. The puppeteer holds the tube beneath the cloth.

3. *Pocket Puppet*—start with a cloth (felt is especially good) or paper pocket (see POCKETS in this section) slightly larger than the child's hand. Round both corners of one end and staple or glue the rounded end and two sides closed, leaving one end open for the hand. Add facial features with markers or use buttons or other discards. Add yarn hair if desired.

Puppet Theatre

Children can install this simple puppet theatre in seconds, and you can make it in minutes. It hangs from the SUSPENSION ROD in a doorway, or on hooks on the wall when not in use. It requires one square yard of vinyl (not clear) such as the kind used for upholstery, two ½" (1.27cm) diameter wooden dowels, 2 cuphooks and a paper stapler. Cut the length 36" (91.4cm) and trim the width slightly narrower than the doorway in which it will be used. Turn down 1½" (3.8cm) hems at the top and bottom. Machine-stitching will hold the hems best, or you may staple them with a paper stapler. Put the staples 2" (5.08cm) apart. Cut a 10" × 16" (25.4cm × 40.6cm) window, 3" (7.62cm) from the top edge after it has been hemmed. Cut the dowels the width of the theatre, and slip them through the hems. Staple through the fabric into the dowels in several places on the backside to hold in place. Screw the two cuphooks into the top dowel, positioning them to fit two of the hooks of the SUSPENSION ROD and centering it in the doorway. To use the theatre, children can fit the SUSPENSION ROD in the upper doorway sockets, (as described under SUSPENSION ROD in PUTTING IT ALL TOGETHER) and hang the theatre from it. When not in use, the theatre can hang on hooks on a wall.

Paper Strips

Level:

Beginning to Advanced

Here are three good activities for students who lack experience with scissors, paper, and glue, no matter what their ages. Cut Strips is especially good for young beginners, but all three are effective for all levels. They all use construction paper strips, ½'' (12.7mm) wide, and in lengths from 6'' (15.2cm) to 18'' (45.7cm). Lighter weight paper is too flimsy and difficult to cut. Place the strips in a container and let students choose the ones they want. Demonstrate the three activities as you introduce them.

1. *Cut Strips*—cut the strips into squares, slowly and deliberately, to gain control of scissors. Cutting is the object of the activity, but if students want to use the cut squares, they can glue them onto paper or a styrofoam tray in their own design.

2. *Arches*—strips in different lengths are glued or taped to construction paper, manila paper, or a shirt cardboard to form arches as shown. Children sometimes call them ''freeways.'' A random over-and-under pattern is used, and some arches may be twisted as they're attached. Holes in the strips made with the hole punch add variety.

3. *Chains*—strips are made into interlocking loops to form chains, by gluing or stapling the ends together.

Clay

It must be true that there is honor even among thieves, because a most considerate one once visited our house. After he had filled one of our suitcases with cameras and other portables, he chose to make his exit through a window which had a row of little clay figures our children and their friends had made drying on the sill. Our Thoughtful Thief moved them all carefully, without damaging a single one. To tell the truth I can't find much relevance to this story, except that it's about clay, which is an important addition to your CONSTRUCTION Area.

Clay is not the same as modeling dough, and nothing will do but real potter's clay. It is a luxury since it's not a reusable commodity. On the other hand, a 25-pound block is not expensive and lasts a long time. I say scrimp on paper if you have to, but have a supply of clay at all times! It is unique as a medium because sculpting is unique; nothing else offers the same opportunity to work in the third dimension. Nothing will do what clay does but clay.

If you are convinced by now, go to a ceramic supply store and ask for red potter's clay. The white kind will do, but it's more expensive. Store the clay carefully to prevent drying out. A small covered plastic garbage can works well; put a wet sponge inside the plastic bag of clay, reclose it and put it in the covered can. Children should ask an adult for a piece of clay when they wish to sculpt. Expect a child's first attempts to be blobs, but have patience—inspired productions will follow. Of course, students provide their own ideas for what to make.

Expect the same children to use clay over and over, while others never touch it. Some respond unusually well to the tactile expression of sculpting and modeling; others are happier with one-dimensional paper activities.

Clay cleanup is best left to adults. Dried clay quickly turns to mud when water is added. Designate a "clay place" and see that clay is never used anywhere else. Tape a piece of heavy plastic on a table space if you like, to reserve the spot for clay. Also designate a drying place for wet creations, because they will soil car upholstery and furniture if taken home in the wet state. Dried pieces (firing is unnecessary) can be painted with easel paint as an option, but since the tactile experience is primary, I do not encourage it unless a child feels his creation is not complete without it.

Painting

Much of preschool painting is experimentation with the medium—spreading paint on paper—and no more. First paintings and drawings will literally be scribbling, and this is exactly as it should be. You will find this particularly true of Beginners and some young Intermediates. Older Intermediates and Advanced students will produce what seem to be warped geometric shapes and, finally, an endless stream of recognizable portrayals of houses, people and animals. Any attempt to hurry children through this development to more sophisticated or realistic representations will be harmful. The simplest line drawings are an important link between children and their surroundings and must be encouraged.

Close to the age of four most children begin to put themselves and others in their paintings and drawings. The pictures often contain a wealth of information about children's internal goings-on. They can be quite personal and deserve the same respect as shared confidences.

Parents value their children's art work and you can make them a gift occasionally by recording stories on the backs of the pictures as the children dictate them to you. Date them, too; it will be appreciated. Sometimes a title will tell a picture's story—"My family at the beach," for example. If the child names the parts— "This is me, this is my sister"—you can label them, if the child wants you to, in lieu of writing a story. Please remember to ask the artist's permission. "May I write about your picture?" or "Do you want to tell me about your picture?" are good approaches. Expect (and respect) an occasional "No." Care must be taken to avoid pressure for the sake of performance. Undue interest from an adult may cause a child to question his work.

Paint is indispensable to art, but unfortunately it is often the first item to be scratched from the list if the budget is tight. But this doesn't mean you can't have paint! You can make your own. It won't have the coverage of commercial tempera, but children are quite satisfied with it, and it can be used freely since it can be made inexpensively. This recipe for paint can also double as fingerpaint (with a slight change in the recipe), and even as paste. You may prefer this homemade paste to the thick kind of school paste which ends up in blobs, or the squeeze bottles of white glue which are maddening when they become clogged. The clogging problem can be avoided by transferring the glue to small juice cans and using brushes with it, but the paste you make yourself is a considerable saving in cost. Here is the recipe for:

All Purpose, Very Good Paint and Paste

3 tablespoons sugar
¼ cup cornstarch
4 cups water
½–1 teaspoon food coloring for
PAINT

Cook til clear. You may add 30 drops oil of cloves as a preservative if you want, but I've never found it necessary. For fingerpaint, double the cornstarch and halve the water. Apply the paste with a brush.

Individualized Painting

Does the idea of individualized painting terrorize you? Do you envision a shambles with a painted child in the center? Forget such fears! It's done on the same basis as all the other activities—responsibility is a prerequisite for participation. Here's the secret—children love to paint, and they will demonstrate whatever self-control is required to participate.

Teachers are almost always surprised by the ease with which individualized painting can be added to a program. It may be hard for you to imagine that four- and five-year-olds, and even some threes, can manage to paint without any help at all from an adult and do it with virtually no mess. You may have to try it to be convinced! Introduce it after your class has become used to other individualized activities, give individual lessons and base participation on readiness. Children should be able to handle all these steps with no interruption to the rhythm of the class:

1. Get a sheet of paper
2. Fasten it to the easel
3. Put on a smock (one which children can put on without assistance)
4. Ask for paint—(one or two colors, a brush for each)
5. Ask an adult to put his name on the painting if he is unable to do it (a crayon on a string attached to the easel is handy)
6. Leave the painting on the easel to dry (this is important to prevent a trail of drips)
7. Return paint and brush(es) to an adult
8. Hang up smock and wash hands

This is a pretty tall order for young children, but I've had many three-year-olds who were sufficiently motivated by their desire to paint master all the steps. This will not be true of all three-year-olds, and, of course, for children under three individualized painting is inappropriate.

If you have no easel, tape a piece of heavy plastic (the kind used for laminating is fine) securely to the wall around all the edges, and let it extend out on the floor 18'' (45.7cm) or so to catch drips. Tape paper to it for painting with masking tape.

Chalkboard

Level:

Beginning to Advanced

For some reason, chalkboards are rare in preschool classrooms. This can be remedied by making your own, which is simpler than you might think. Chalkboard paint is available anywhere paint is sold, and two coats of it on any smooth surface magically produces a chalkboard. A door is one possibility; so is a piece of smooth hardboard (Masonite) attached to the wall. Actually, the smooth side of hardboard makes a pretty good chalkboard as is. Season it or a newly painted chalkboard by covering it completely with chalk (used sideways), and erasing it. White chalk is fine, or you may provide colored sticks, though I prefer to use these for sidewalk murals outdoors. Store chalk out of reach, if you need to, and let children ask for it when they want to make chalk pictures. A dry poly sponge makes a good eraser.

Junk Sculpture

Level:

Intermediate to Advanced

Junk can make a marvelous contribution to creativity. In spite of the shaky appearance of the junk sculpture, no other medium offers the same experience with balance and design, weight and proportion. Junking couldn't be easier so long as you can keep a constant flow of material coming in. Parents will usually be happy to cooperate. Junk is similar to collage materials, but larger in size, as it is used for three-dimensional construction. It may not be suitable for daily use because of the tremendous spread of truly inventive junking, but it's too fine an activity to give up. Collect junk and bring it out for a day or two until all who wish have participated, then return it to storage, to be replenished and brought out again later. Paste made from the recipe in this chapter won't work with junk creations; white glue is needed. Masking tape is almost a necessity; a staff member will have to be on hand during sessions to give short strips as needed. Good junk might include:

1. cardboard boxes, to be used as a base for sculpture
2. parts from discarded clocks, radios, cameras, etc. (Children will gladly dismantle these, if they are given screwdrivers.)
3. wood scraps, fabric scraps, carpet scraps
4. yarn, string
5. any discarded hardware items, if safe
6. plastic bottles, caps
7. cardboard, paper, tissue
8. paper rolls from paper towels, tissue
9. wire of all kinds
10. plastic scraps of all kinds
11. fur, leather scraps
12. building materials of all kinds, if safe

Yarn

Level:

Intermediate to Advanced

Yarn is such an important staple, I hope you have some staff members and parents with needlecraft hobbies who will save their leftover yarn for you. Roll it into balls or wind it on cardboard rolls (cut a slit in one edge for the end of the yarn). Skeins and children are an impossible combination—they can tangle a skein of yarn faster than kittens. Put the yarn supply in an ice cream tub or other container and leave it out for everyday use.

Finger Weaving

Level:

Intermediate to Advanced

This is a lot of fun to do and requires no tools of any kind. Scrap yarn or string of all kinds can be used (tie them together for a good effect), or if you're starting from scratch, buy thick rug yarn. Teach a few children how to finger weave (they will teach others) and soon you'll have chains everywhere. For several years long fingerwoven ropes decorated our Christmas trees. Children like to make chains on car trips, too. It's really a crochet chain stitch done without a hook, but you don't need to know how to crochet to teach it or to learn it. It's much easier to do than to read about, so you can learn it best by trying it.

Tie a loop the size of a quarter in one end of a length of yarn. Slip the loop over the thumb and forefinger of your dominant hand and hold the yarn a short distance from the loop with the other hand. *Reaching through the loop* with your thumb and forefinger, grasp the yarn and pull it through the loop to make another loop the size of a quarter. Now slip through the new loop and grasp the yarn again, make another loop, and keep repeating the steps. That's all there is to it. Chains may be woven loosely or tightly. After they have mastered the basic steps, children may find it helps to keep a bit of tension on the yarn with the holding (non-dominant) hand,

so if they like, they can loop it around the fingers of that hand any way that feels comfortable.

The best way to teach finger weaving to children is with an unhurried "watch me" session. Sit in the middle of a group and let them watch while you make a chain. If you have some end-looped lengths of yarn at hand, they will pick them up and begin weaving when they are ready.

Batik

Level:

Intermediate to Advanced

These dip prints are always a surprise—each one is different. You need 3 or 4 different food colors, a 6-cup muffin tin and white paper towels. A colored water solution, much stronger than the one for exercises in which coloring facilitates viewing, is necessary to produce rich-hued designs. If you like, mix small squeeze bottles of colored water to have on hand and add approximately a tablespoon of each to the muffin tin when a child wants to make a batik. Store the towels and muffin tin on the shelf and the colored water separately. Help a few children make batiks and they can teach others. Here's how:

Fan-fold a paper towel crosswise or lengthwise in approximately 1½'' (3.81cm) folds, stacking the folds as you go. There are two ways to proceed from here:

1. A 3-cornered fold, which is slightly more difficult but makes a more interesting design when dipped, or,
2. A 4-cornered fold, which is easier to make, and produces a simpler, but attractive, design. Teach either or both folds.

Three cornered: Starting at one end of the stacked ''fan'', fold one corner in a triangle approximately the same size as the width of the fan-folds. Then fold it backwards in the opposite direction, stacking the folds. Continue folding to the end, alternating each time—the way a flag is folded—ending with a triangle.

Four-cornered: Start at one end of the ''fan'' and fold across approximately 1½'' (3.81cm) from the end (the same width as the fan). Repeat, folding over and over to the end, ending with a square.

To dip either kind of fold: Dip each corner in a different color (3 for three-cornered; 4 for four-cornered) in the muffin tin, allowing it to soak only the corner—leave some white in the middle. Unfold carefully, and lay out to dry. I think students should be allowed to make at least two—they're like eating peanuts!

Incidentally, a drying space is needed in the CONSTRUCTION area for all wet work which can be moved. (BOX PAINTING and EASEL PAINTING should stay in place until dry.) An activity is not finished until all materials, including the finished product, have been removed from the work place. Expect students to put away what they've made, either in their personal storage spaces if it's dry, or in the designated drying place, if it's wet.

Discards

Level:

Beginning to Advanced

Children are most inventive when materials are close at hand, enabling them to translate ideas into action without delay. A plentiful supply of discards will fill many inventive needs. They will frequently add the finishing touches when children are ''making things,'' making puppets, or working with wood; they also stretch the imagination beyond the limitations of the usual paper, paste and crayons.

Junk and collage discards may double for these other purposes if you like, or you may have a separate supply. Encourage everyone to catch the discard spirit and to save for the collection. In addition to the items suggested for COLLAGE and JUNK, examine everything for creative potential before throwing it away—you never know what will spark ideas.

You've probably already discovered that magazines and newspapers are handy for many purposes. In case you haven't, a stack of magazines will supply students with varied cutting opportunities, and the cutouts will find their way into all kinds of construction projects. Newspapers are indispensable for use under painting projects, and for making puppets.

People Pictures

Level:

Intermediate with
assistance, Advanced

If you have a roll of butcher paper, as I suggest under "MAKING THINGS", you can make people pictures. Help the first few children make theirs; the children can help each other thereafter. Tear off a sheet of butcher paper slightly longer than the child is tall and have her lie down on it on the floor. Trace around her with a black crayon. Let her add the details to make her look as she does that day, using crayons, paint, markers, or all three. Roll the picture to take home when it is dry. She may want to tape it to her bedroom door. She can measure herself by it later and see how she's grown, so dating it will be appreciated.

Box Painting

Level:

Beginning to Advanced

Painting a surface in order to cover it is a different experience from painting a picture, and children love it. Box painting is too expensive if tempera is used, but All-Purpose Paint, made by the recipe in this section, can be used freely. Provide a 1'' (2.5cm) or 1½'' (3.8cm) wide brush (the hardware variety) and one color of paint in a small juice can. The painter wears a smock, and returns the paint and brush to an adult when the box is finished, or the painter is, whichever happens first. Remind students to put the box on newspaper before beginning, and to leave it there to dry. What to do with dry painted boxes? Ask the painters frankly if they want to keep them. In most cases the answer will be no and they can be discarded, or if a box was only partially painted, it can be put back in the collection to be finished by someone else.

Box Wrapping

Level:

Intermediate to Advanced

Collect little boxes, child's shoe box size and smaller, and used wrapping paper, ribbon and bows. Parents will be obliging if you add these to your ''need'' list. Keep the boxes in a large box (covered with wrapping paper to indicate the activity if you like) or use a joint collection for box painting and box wrapping. Store wrappings in a container nearby. Children may ask for cellophane tape if it's available or they can use glue or paste if it's not. Tape the boxes securely closed before adding them to the collections; otherwise, children sometimes put small parts of learning materials inside. They may keep the wrapped boxes or give them to each other.

Woodworking

Level:

Intermediate to
Advanced, with close
supervision

I hope you won't think of woodworking as optional. No individualized program is complete without it. You can chart gains in fine-motor development from the beginning of the year to the end by observing the children working with tools and wood.

Children learn something else just as important as manual dexterity through their woodworking: they develop a knowledge of and a respect for tools. Hammers and saws make no exceptions for lack of experience. But competency with them can be acquired, and therein lies the secret to handling them safely. Tools perform only as they are directed, no more and no less, so learning to make them work for you is a heady accomplishment. And tools being the unforgiving things they are, cooperating with them is one's wisest alternative—a concept which is readily appreciated by even the youngest children.

You may choose to make woodworking a once-or twice-a-week activity rather than a daily one, since it requires close adult supervision, but if you make it available less often than weekly, it will be so popular that mayhem will ensue each time. Better to make it as much a regular part of the schedule as possible. Don't avoid it for safety reasons, but keep watch when the tools are in use and require shoes to be worn by the workers.

Woodworking is a bit different from the other individualized activities, since students work on separate projects, but they share the tools, as several different ones may be needed by each child.

The objective is not "making something" but "doing something", so suggestions to make things such as airplanes, boats, etc., would defeat the purpose. Expect a lot of aimless hammering and hacking at first. Even later, you'll be disappointed if you expect recognizable replicas of real objects. We have enough airplanes and boats, made mostly by machines, but your children's creations will be true hand-crafted originals. Nameless, as a rule—but beautiful because they're one of a kind.

Besides wood scraps, which parents will usually donate if asked, string, yarn, wire, carpet scraps, sandpaper, etc. will inspire ideas. Balsa is a gift from heaven.

As for nails, the larger the head the better the target. None should be shorter than 1'' (2.5cm) or so, and definitely no tacks. Keep in mind:

1. A workbench is the ultimate, of course, but an old, low, sturdy table will suffice, or the floor can be used.
2. If woodworking is done on the floor, continual checking for nails is necessary.
3. Limit the number working at one time to a small enough group that you can watch them all closely with ease.
4. Children love sawing, but it's tricky. A small vise on the workbench or table will hold the piece steady as it's being cut.
5. Small blocks and scraps are more manageable than large pieces.
6. Store nails away from children's reach when not in use.

These are the tools you will need:

1. hammers—2 or 3—small adult size, not toys
2. saws—1 or 2—small adult size
3. a small hand drill—adult

Whether or not you allow easel paint as an adjunct to workworking is up to you. Some children may feel their construction isn't complete without it.

A piece of pegboard on the wall works well for both display and storage of tools. Outline the tools with a marker, and if necessary, remove them from the pegboard when you don't want them in use.

Workworking for Beginners

Small hammers are safe for Beginners with close supervison. A good Beginner's activity is hammering golf tees into soft ceiling tile. Blunt the ends of the tees by rubbing them over sandpaper, holding them straight up and down. Older beginners may use nails with close supervision. Make sure the nails are shorter than the depth of the tile, to prevent damage to the floor. Buy ceiling tile in a 2' × 4' (61cm × 122cm) sheet at a hardware store or home center and cut it with a sharp knife into 12'' (30.5cm) squares. Glue two or more thicknesses together with contact cement or other glue to achieve the right thickness. Both sides can be used. Do this activity on the floor to prevent damage to tables. Golf tees and nails can be removed from the tile and reused many times.

Tissue Mosaic

Level:

Intermediate to
Advanced

Tissue mosaics are not made from discards, but they are such a great activity they're worth the investment in colored tissue. Tissue goes a long way; small pieces are used for mosaics, so it's economical in the long run. Children never seem to tire of making these—each one is different. The colors are vibrant and satisfying and it's a can't-miss project.

Fill a large container with small-to-medium pieces of torn tissue (if children redesign the pieces to their satisfaction, so much the better), and put it on the shelf. Children ask for glue or paste from the recipe given in this section to make a mosaic. The backing can be paper, cardboard or styro trays: white is best. Pieces of tissue are attached by brushing white glue over them (or glue diluted ½ with water). Cover the pieces entirely; the glue soaks through the tissue and adheres it to the backing. The idea is to overlap edges, thereby producing other colors, so the pieces should be crowded close together. The colors are almost transparent when dry and resemble stained glass. Details may be added, or the edges of the tissue outlined with black marker when the mosaics are completely dry.

Buy tissue at a variety store, school supply or art supply, in packages of assorted colors.

"Making Things"

The suggested construction activities are only starters—they are by no means intended to rule out free construction—"making things." Children's own inventions must always be encouraged. Never mind that they're not objects to treasure, or that they may end up underfoot before the day is over. They are part of a process. Put these basic supplies on the workshelf in the construction area to be used freely, along with the other art activities.

1. A small container with several pairs of scissors. It's absolutely vital to have good ones; try them yourself first. Intermediate and Advanced students can use semi-pointed child's scissors (which cut far better than the rounded ones) with supervision. Beginners use good quality rounded scissors.
2. A container with 2 or 3 glue cans: white glue or paste from the recipe given in this section in small frozen juice cans, with a stiff brush in each one. Remind students to keep brushes in the glue to prevent them from drying out.
3. A container of crayons. I prefer large crayons in the eight basic colors for all ages, but use whatever kind you prefer. I like to have them sorted by colors in a muffin tin, which can be carried to the workspace. There is no need to have all 8 colors available at one time. Preschool children are not yet color/reality conscious: they make pink trees and blue dogs with carefree abandon. Limiting the number of colors eliminates the distraction of too many choices. Rotate them, using 3 or 4 colors at a time. Some Advanced students may have developed color consciousness; if they request more colors it's because they are ready for them, so they should be given.
4. I heartily recommend a set of non-toxic, washable broad-tip markers to be used with discretion, especially by Advanced students. They can't be left on the shelf for general use, but keep them stored elsewhere and let them be used by individuals who request them, after they prove their ability to use them responsibly and return them to you.
5. Stapler. The same goes for a stapler. It performs so many construction jobs that can't be done by any other means that it's really a shame not to have one. It

opens doors to a whole new range of art projects which children will discover for themselves. Get one which is simple to operate, even a tot (tiny one), and make it available on the same basis as the markers.

6. Tape. Cellophane and masking—these are real luxuries but if you should have a benefactor in the person of a parent who is a stationer, for instance, count yourself lucky and enjoy! Students can use tape on the same basis as the stapler and markers, with one exception: they are often able to use tape appropriately before they are able to tear it off in short pieces. The solution is for a staff member to tear off strips and attach them to the table edge near the child's work.

7. Styrofoam trays. A large container can hold styrofoam trays (prepackaged meat comes in these) in all sizes. They will be used as backing for collages and pictures and many other things.

8. Paper hole punch. This is optional but it does add possibilities for exploring with paper.

9. Paper
a. Colored construction paper—if it is available for free construction. If not, scraps of construction paper from other class projects. Save them faithfully and put them in a large container. (Ice cream stores will save large round cartons if you ask.)
b. White paper—newsprint is traditional. Cut it into halves and fourths and have stacks on a tray or in a shallow container for crayon work, etc. Whole sheets are needed for painting.

Paper is indispensable for art, of course, and unfortunately is an ongoing expense. Rather than severely limit its use, if the expense is a problem, seek other solutions. Stationery stores and printers often throw away all kinds of colored and white paper trimmings, many large enough for use by schools. They may save several days' supply for you if you ask. Also consider buying a roll of butcher (market) paper from an office supply. It's by far the most economical way to have an abundant supply of paper. It can be used for any project which usually requires newsprint or manila paper. Treat yourself to a holder, too—it will have a cutter which will save you time and frustration.

Displaying

It's often tempting for us to select pieces of students' art work that we consider outstanding, and display them as a form of encouragement. This can have the opposite effect, however. Children may interpret it to mean we especially like those techniques or subjects, and since our approval is important to them, they may reproduce variations of them again and again, interrupting their experimentation and creative growth. This raises the question of whether it is in creativity's best interest to display children's art at all. The answer lies in the motivation behind displaying: whether it is to please observers (adults) or creators (children). Children have no interest in seeing their work displayed. How often do you find a piece of art work, which only minutes ago was the object of deep concentration, crumpled in the wastebasket? It is adults who value finished products. Children value the process. They do observe that displaying their work seems to please adults, which explains why they sometimes want it "put up", but rarely is the idea their own. Even when they do develop a deep attachment to something they've made, they still have no interest in seeing it displayed. As a matter of fact, they may resent making it "public property." Either they feel neutral about it or they want it all to themselves.

As for encouragement, children will sense it in your efforts toward keeping materials generously supplied. They will know instinctively they have your approval to create freely and expressively. The implication is: don't attach an assumed importance to children's handiwork; more than likely it was a part of a process, important at the moment of execution, but not longer. They can do a dozen more.

Epilogue

Cassandra's Story

Once, when I taught third grade, I gave my class an English test, covering usage of the "helping" words *has* and *hasn't, have* and *haven't, had* and *hadn't.* I expected a brief explanation of their usage with certain verbs in the past tense. From Cassandra I received:

> You use *have* when you don't use *has.* You use *has* when you shouldn't use *had.* You use *had* when you can't use *have.* You use *haven't* when you haven't used *haven't.* You use *hasn't* if it's not *hadn't* or *haven't.* You use *hadn't* when you're supposed to.

I learned several things about learning from this exchange.

First, the dark side: I felt somehow guilty of entrapment. I knew Cassandra's spoken grammar was fine. Was the complication of putting it to the test really necessary—or even justifiable? I winced at her obvious bewilderment and decided there had to be a better way for two people to exchange information than a showdown.

But on the bright side: I wonder how Cassandra has fared in the ensuing years and decide that her inventiveness and perseverance have probably served her well and that cheers me somewhat.

The dark side again: I felt my only recourse was to give the paper a failing grade, but it was the finest piece of creative writing I received all year. Now does that make sense?

But, the bright side: Cassandra's story is not yet ended. We both failed that English test but it helped clarify in my mind what education isn't, so all was not lost.

Perhaps children need advocates more than experts since expertise is so undependable. Education is every bit as fickle as fashion. What experts decree as highly relevant today may be hardly recognized tomorrow and supplanted altogether the day after. So an advocate's unwavering defense of children's essential humanness may be the only real constant. Pedagogy may sometimes fail children, but an advocate never will.

Story S-t-r-e-t-c-h-e-r-s®:
Activities to Expand Children's Favorite Books (Pre-K and K)

Shirley C. Raines and Robert J. Canady

It's original. It's fun. It's 450 terrific teaching ideas that are based upon the latest research on how young children become good readers. It connects 90 of the best children's books to every learning center science, nature, math, art, music, movement, cooking, circle time.

Each book is "stretched" five ways with lively learning activities that heighten reading readiness and sharpen comprehension skills, too. And it's so easy to use! 256 pages.

ISBN 0-87659-119-5   **Gryphon House**
10011   **Paperback**

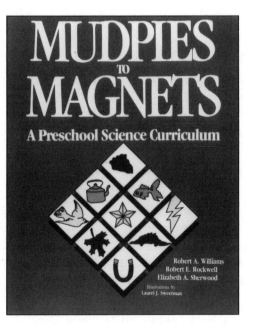

Mudpies to Magnets
A Preschool Science Curriculum

Robert A. Williams, Robert E. Rockwell, and Elizabeth A. Sherwood, Illustrated by Laurel Sweetman

These 112 science experiments cover a wide range of topics, include the repetition that is needed for mastery and occur in a sequence that provides for growth and development. From "Pill Bug Palaces" to "Let's Get Soaked," the experiments here will delight and amaze children. 154 pages.

ISBN 0-87659-112-8   **Gryphon House**
10005   **Paperback**

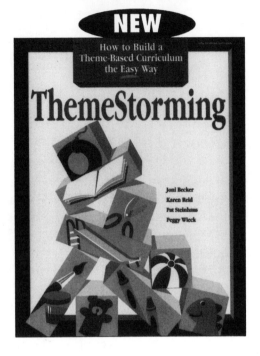

Themestorming: How To Build Your Own Theme-Oriented Curriculum the Easy way

Joni Becker, Karen Reid, Pat Steinhaus and Peggy Wieck

A complete theme activity book with everything you need to know about ten popular themes, from learning center and snack suggestions; to discovery, art, music and movement, math and language activities. Also included for each theme are transition ideas, songs and chants, theme extensions and variations, and a bibliography. The quick and easy activities all relate to the theme. Themes include Sticky; Muddy Puddles, Soap and Bubbles; Meanies, Monsters and Make-Believe; and Surprises and Celebrations.

ISBN 0-87659-170-5   **Gryphon House**
18574   **Paperback**

The Peaceful Classroom
162 Easy Activities to Teach Preschoolers Compassion and Cooperation

Charles Smith, Ph.D

Compassion, cooperation, friendship and respect for others are important to the development of every human being. **The Peaceful Classroom** is filled with appealing group learning activities which help children acquire these skills. The book also suggests ways teachers can work with parents to extend these learning experiences at home. A timely and important resource for every classroom. 208 pages.

ISBN 0-87659-165-9   **Gryphon House**
15186   **Paperback**